OTHELLO

William Shakespeare

D0047180

SPARK PUBLISHING

122 Fifth Avenue
New York, NY 10011
www.sparknotes.com

ISBN 978-1-4114-6962-4

Please submit changes or report errors to www.sparknotes.com/errors.

Printed in Canada

10 9 8 7 6 5 4 3 2 1

CONTENTS

CONTEXT

HE MOST INFLUENTIAL WRITER in all of English literature, William Shakespeare was born in 1564 to a successful middle-class glove-maker in Stratford-upon-Avon, England. Shakespeare attended grammar school, but his formal education proceeded no further. In 1582 he married an older woman, Anne Hathaway, and had three children with her. Around 1590 he left his family behind and traveled to London to work as an actor and playwright. Public and critical acclaim quickly followed, and Shakespeare eventually became the most popular playwright in England and part-owner of the Globe Theater. His career bridged the reigns of Elizabeth I (ruled 1558–1603) and James I (ruled 1603–1625), and he was a favorite of both monarchs. Indeed, James granted Shakespeare's company the greatest possible compliment by bestowing upon its members the title of King's Men. Wealthy and renowned, Shakespeare retired to Stratford and died in 1616 at the age of fifty-two. At the time of Shakespeare's death, literary luminaries such as Ben Jonson hailed his works as timeless.

Shakespeare's works were collected and printed in various editions in the century following his death, and by the early eighteenth century his reputation as the greatest poet ever to write in English was well established. The unprecedented admiration garnered by his works led to a fierce curiosity about Shakespeare's life, but the dearth of biographical information has left many details of Shakespeare's personal history shrouded in mystery. Some people have concluded from this fact and from Shakespeare's modest education that Shakespeare's plays were actually written by someone else—Francis Bacon and the Earl of Oxford are the two most popular candidates—but the support for this claim is overwhelmingly circumstantial, and the theory is not taken seriously by many scholars.

In the absence of credible evidence to the contrary, Shakespeare must be viewed as the author of the thirty-seven plays and 154 sonnets that bear his name. The legacy of this body of work is immense. A number of Shakespeare's plays seem to have transcended even the category of brilliance, becoming so influential as to affect profoundly the course of Western literature and culture ever after.

ONTEXT

I

Othello was first performed by the King's Men at the court of King James I on November 1, 1604. Written during Shakespeare's great tragic period, which also included the composition of *Hamlet* (1600), *King Lear* (1604–5), *Macbeth* (1606), and *Antony and Cleopatra* (1606–7), *Othello* is set against the backdrop of the wars between Venice and Turkey that raged in the latter part of the sixteenth century. Cyprus, which is the setting for most of the action, was a Venetian outpost attacked by the Turks in 1570 and conquered the following year. Shakespeare's information on the Venetian-Turkish conflict probably derives from *The History of the Turks* by Richard Knolles, which was published in England in the autumn of 1603. The story of *Othello* is also derived from another source—an Italian prose tale written in 1565 by Giovanni Battista Giraldi Cinzio (usually referred to as Cinthio). The original story contains the bare bones of Shakespeare's plot: a Moorish general is deceived by his ensign into believing his wife is unfaithful. To Cinthio's story Shakespeare added supporting characters such as the rich young dupe Roderigo and the outraged and grief-stricken Brabanzio, Desdemona's father. Shakespeare compressed the action into the space of a few days and set it against the backdrop of military conflict. And, most memorably, he turned the ensign, a minor villain, into the arch-villain Iago.

The question of Othello's exact race is open to some debate. The word Moor now refers to the Islamic Arabic inhabitants of North Africa who conquered Spain in the eighth century, but the term was used rather broadly in the period and was sometimes applied to Africans from other regions. George Abbott, for example, in his *A Brief Description of the Whole World* of 1599, made distinctions between "blackish Moors" and "black Negroes"; a 1600 translation of John Leo's *The History and Description of Africa* distinguishes "white or tawny Moors" of the Mediterranean coast of Africa from the "Negroes or black Moors" of the south. Othello's darkness or blackness is alluded to many times in the play, but Shakespeare and other Elizabethans frequently described brunette or darker than average Europeans as black. The opposition of black and white imagery that runs throughout *Othello* is certainly a marker of difference between Othello and his European peers, but the difference is never quite so racially specific as a modern reader might imagine it to be.

While Moor characters abound on the Elizabethan and Jacobean stage, none are given so major or heroic a role as Othello. Perhaps the most vividly stereotypical black character of the period is Aaron, the villain of Shakespeare's early play *Titus Andronicus*. The antithesis of Othello, Aaron is lecherous, cunning, and vicious; his final words are: "If one good deed in all my life I did / I do repent it to my very soul" (*Titus Andronicus,* V.iii.188–189). Othello, by contrast, is a noble figure of great authority, respected and admired by the duke and senate of Venice as well as by those who serve him, such as Cassio, Montano, and Lodovico. Only Iago voices an explicitly stereotypical view of Othello, depicting him from the beginning as an animalistic, barbarous, foolish outsider.

CONTEXT

PLOT OVERVIEW

Othello begins on a street in Venice, in the midst of an argument between Roderigo, a rich man, and Iago. Roderigo has been paying Iago to help him in his suit to Desdemona. But Roderigo has just learned that Desdemona has married Othello, a general whom Iago begrudgingly serves as ensign. Iago says he hates Othello, who recently passed him over for the position of lieutenant in favor of the inexperienced soldier Michael Cassio.

Unseen, Iago and Roderigo cry out to Brabanzio that his daughter Desdemona has been stolen by and married to Othello, the Moor. Brabanzio finds that his daughter is indeed missing, and he gathers some officers to find Othello. Not wanting his hatred of Othello to be known, Iago leaves Roderigo and hurries back to Othello before Brabanzio sees him. At Othello's lodgings, Cassio arrives with an urgent message from the duke: Othello's help is needed in the matter of the imminent Turkish invasion of Cyprus. Not long afterward, Brabanzio arrives with Roderigo and others, and accuses Othello of stealing his daughter by witchcraft. When he finds out that Othello is on his way to speak with the duke, Brabanzio decides to go along and accuse Othello before the assembled senate.

Brabanzio's plan backfires. The duke and senate are very sympathetic toward Othello. Given a chance to speak for himself, Othello explains that he wooed and won Desdemona not by witchcraft but with the stories of his adventures in travel and war. The duke finds Othello's explanation convincing, and Desdemona herself enters at this point to defend her choice in marriage and to announce to her father that her allegiance is now to her husband. Brabanzio is frustrated, but acquiesces and allows the senate meeting to resume. The duke says that Othello must go to Cyprus to aid in the defense against the Turks, who are headed for the island. Desdemona insists that she accompany her husband on his trip, and preparations are made for them to depart that night.

In Cyprus the following day, two gentlemen stand on the shore with Montano, the governor of Cyprus. A third gentleman arrives and reports that the Turkish fleet has been wrecked in a storm at sea. Cassio, whose ship did not suffer the same fate, arrives soon after, followed by a second ship carrying Iago, Roderigo, Desdemona, and

Emilia, Iago's wife. Once they have landed, Othello's ship is sighted, and the group goes to the harbor. As they wait for Othello, Cassio greets Desdemona by clasping her hand. Watching them, Iago tells the audience that he will use "as little a web as this" hand-holding to ensnare Cassio (II.i.169).

Othello arrives, greets his wife, and announces that there will be reveling that evening to celebrate Cyprus's safety from the Turks. Once everyone has left, Roderigo complains to Iago that he has no chance of breaking up Othello's marriage. Iago assures Roderigo that as soon as Desdemona's "blood is made dull with the act of sport," she will lose interest in Othello and seek sexual satisfaction elsewhere (II.i.222). However, Iago warns that "elsewhere" will likely be with Cassio. Iago counsels Roderigo that he should cast Cassio into disgrace by starting a fight with Cassio at the evening's revels. In a soliloquy, Iago explains to the audience that eliminating Cassio is the first crucial step in his plan to ruin Othello. That night, Iago gets Cassio drunk and then sends Roderigo to start a fight with him. Apparently provoked by Roderigo, Cassio chases Roderigo across the stage. Governor Montano attempts to hold Cassio down, and Cassio stabs him. Iago sends Roderigo to raise alarm in the town.

The alarm is rung, and Othello, who had left earlier with plans to consummate his marriage, soon arrives to still the commotion. When Othello demands to know who began the fight, Iago feigns reluctance to implicate his "friend" Cassio, but he ultimately tells the whole story. Othello then strips Cassio of his rank of lieutenant. Cassio is extremely upset, and he laments to Iago, once everyone else has gone, that his reputation has been ruined forever. Iago assures Cassio that he can get back into Othello's good graces by using Desdemona as an intermediary. In a soliloquy, Iago tells us that he will frame Cassio and Desdemona as lovers to make Othello jealous.

In an attempt at reconciliation, Cassio sends some musicians to play beneath Othello's window. Othello, however, sends his clown to tell the musicians to go away. Hoping to arrange a meeting with Desdemona, Cassio asks the clown, a peasant who serves Othello, to send Emilia to him. After the clown departs, Iago passes by and tells Cassio that he will get Othello out of the way so that Cassio can speak privately with Desdemona. Othello, Iago, and a gentleman go to examine some of the town's fortifications.

Desdemona is quite sympathetic to Cassio's request and promises that she will do everything she can to make Othello forgive his former lieutenant. As Cassio is about to leave, Othello and Iago return. Feeling uneasy, Cassio leaves without talking to Othello. Othello inquires whether it was Cassio who just parted from his wife, and Iago, beginning to kindle Othello's fire of jealousy, replies, "No, sure, I cannot think it, / That he would steal away so guilty-like, / Seeing your coming" (III.iii.37–39).

Othello becomes upset and moody, and Iago furthers his goal of removing both Cassio and Othello by suggesting that Cassio and Desdemona are involved in an affair. Desdemona's entreaties to Othello to reinstate Cassio as lieutenant add to Othello's almost immediate conviction that his wife is unfaithful. After Othello's conversation with Iago, Desdemona comes to call Othello to supper and finds him feeling unwell. She offers him her handkerchief to wrap around his head, but he finds it to be "[t]oo little" and lets it drop to the floor (III.iii.291). Desdemona and Othello go to dinner, and Emilia picks up the handkerchief, mentioning to the audience that Iago has always wanted her to steal it for him.

Iago is ecstatic when Emilia gives him the handkerchief, which he plants in Cassio's room as "evidence" of his affair with Desdemona. When Othello demands "ocular proof" (III.iii.365) that his wife is unfaithful, Iago says that he has seen Cassio "wipe his beard" (III.iii.444) with Desdemona's handkerchief—the first gift Othello ever gave her. Othello vows to take vengeance on his wife and on Cassio, and Iago vows that he will help him. When Othello sees Desdemona later that evening, he demands the handkerchief of her, but she tells him that she does not have it with her and attempts to change the subject by continuing her suit on Cassio's behalf. This drives Othello into a further rage, and he storms out. Later, Cassio comes onstage, wondering about the handkerchief he has just found in his chamber. He is greeted by Bianca, a prostitute, whom he asks to take the handkerchief and copy its embroidery for him.

Through Iago's machinations, Othello becomes so consumed by jealousy that he falls into a trance and has a fit of epilepsy. As he writhes on the ground, Cassio comes by, and Iago tells him to come back in a few minutes to talk. Once Othello recovers, Iago tells him of the meeting he has planned with Cassio. He instructs Othello to hide nearby and watch as Iago extracts from Cassio the story of his affair with Desdemona. While Othello stands out of earshot, Iago pumps Cassio for information about Bianca, causing Cassio to laugh and confirm Othello's suspicions. Bianca herself then enters with Desdemona's handkerchief, reprimanding Cassio for making her copy out the embroidery of a love token given to him by another woman. When Desdemona enters with Lodovico and Lodovico subsequently gives Othello a letter from Venice calling him home and instating Cassio as his replacement, Othello goes over the edge, striking Desdemona and then storming out.

That night, Othello accuses Desdemona of being a whore. He ignores her protestations, seconded by Emilia, that she is innocent. Iago assures Desdemona that Othello is simply upset about matters of state. Later that night, however, Othello ominously tells Desdemona to wait for him in bed and to send Emilia away. Meanwhile, Iago assures the still-complaining Roderigo that everything is going as planned: in order to prevent Desdemona and Othello from leaving, Roderigo must kill Cassio. Then he will have a clear avenue to his love.

Iago instructs Roderigo to ambush Cassio, but Roderigo misses his mark and Cassio wounds him instead. Iago wounds Cassio and runs away. When Othello hears Cassio's cry, he assumes that Iago has killed Cassio as he said he would. Lodovico and Graziano enter to see what the commotion is about. Iago enters shortly thereafter and flies into a pretend rage as he "discovers" Cassio's assailant Roderigo, whom he murders. Cassio is taken to have his wound dressed.

Meanwhile, Othello stands over his sleeping wife in their bedchamber, preparing to kill her. Desdemona wakes and attempts to plead with Othello. She asserts her innocence, but Othello smothers her. Emilia enters with the news that Roderigo is dead. Othello asks if Cassio is dead too and is mortified when Emilia says he is not. After crying out that she has been murdered, Desdemona changes her story before she dies, claiming that she has committed suicide. Emilia asks Othello what happened, and Othello tells her that he has killed Desdemona for her infidelity, which Iago brought to his attention.

Montano, Graziano, and Iago come into the room. Iago attempts to silence Emilia, who realizes what Iago has done. At first, Othello insists that Iago has told the truth, citing the handkerchief as evidence. Once Emilia tells him how she found the handkerchief and gave it to Iago, Othello is crushed and begins to weep. He tries to kill Iago but is disarmed. Iago kills Emilia and flees, but he is caught by Lodovico and Montano, who return holding Iago captive. They also bring Cassio, who is now in a chair because of his wound. Othello wounds Iago and is disarmed. Lodovico tells Othello that he must come with them back to Venice to be tried. Othello makes a speech about how he would like to be remembered, then kills himself with a sword he had hidden on his person. The play closes with a speech by Lodovico. He gives Othello's house and goods to Graziano and orders that Iago be executed.

CHARACTER LIST

Othello   The play's protagonist and hero. A Christian Moor and general of the armies of Venice, Othello is an eloquent and physically powerful figure, respected by all those around him. In spite of his elevated status, he is nevertheless easy prey to insecurities because of his age, his life as a soldier, and his race. He possesses a "free and open nature," which his ensign Iago uses to twist his love for his wife, Desdemona, into a powerful and destructive jealousy (I.iii.381).

Desdemona   The daughter of the Venetian senator Brabanzio. Desdemona and Othello are secretly married before the play begins. While in many ways stereotypically pure and meek, Desdemona is also determined and self-possessed. She is equally capable of defending her marriage, jesting bawdily with Iago, and responding with dignity to Othello's incomprehensible jealousy.

Iago   Othello's ensign (a job also known as an ancient or standard-bearer), and the villain of the play. Iago is twenty-eight years old. While his ostensible reason for desiring Othello's demise is that he has been passed over for promotion to lieutenant, Iago's motivations are never very clearly expressed and seem to originate in an obsessive, almost aesthetic delight in manipulation and destruction.

Michael Cassio   Othello's lieutenant. Cassio is a young and inexperienced soldier, whose high position is much resented by Iago. Truly devoted to Othello, Cassio is extremely ashamed after being implicated in a drunken brawl on Cyprus and losing his place as lieutenant. Iago uses Cassio's youth, good looks, and friendship with Desdemona to play on Othello's insecurities about Desdemona's fidelity.

Emilia   Iago's wife and Desdemona's attendant. A cynical, worldly woman, she is deeply attached to her mistress and distrustful of her husband.

Roderigo A jealous suitor of Desdemona. Young, rich, and foolish, Roderigo is convinced that if he gives Iago all of his money, Iago will help him win Desdemona's hand. Repeatedly frustrated as Othello marries Desdemona and then takes her to Cyprus, Roderigo is ultimately desperate enough to agree to help Iago kill Cassio after Iago points out that Cassio is another potential rival for Desdemona.

Bianca   A courtesan, or prostitute, in Cyprus. Bianca's favorite customer is Cassio, who teases her with promises of marriage.

Brabanzio Desdemona's father, a somewhat blustering and self-important Venetian senator. As a friend of Othello, Brabanzio feels betrayed when the general marries his daughter in secret.

Duke of Venice The official authority in Venice, the duke has great respect for Othello as a public and military servant. His primary role within the play is to reconcile Othello and Brabanzio in Act I, scene iii, and then to send Othello to Cyprus.

Montano   The governor of Cyprus before Othello. We see him first in Act II, as he recounts the status of the war and awaits the Venetian ships.

Lodovico One of Brabanzio's kinsmen, Lodovico acts as a messenger from Venice to Cyprus. He arrives in Cyprus in Act IV with letters announcing that Othello has been replaced by Cassio as governor.

Graziano Brabanzio's kinsman who accompanies Lodovico to Cyprus. Amidst the chaos of the final scene, Graziano mentions that Desdemona's father has died.

Clown   Othello's servant. Although the clown appears only in two short scenes, his appearances reflect and distort the action and words of the main plots: his puns on the word "lie" in Act III, scene iv, for example, anticipate Othello's confusion of two meanings of that word in Act IV, scene i.

ANALYSIS OF MAJOR CHARACTERS

OTHELLO

Beginning with the opening lines of the play, Othello remains at a distance from much of the action that concerns and affects him. Roderigo and Iago refer ambiguously to a "he" or "him" for much of the first scene. When they begin to specify whom they are talking about, especially once they stand beneath Brabanzio's window, they do so with racial epithets, not names. These include "the Moor" (I.i.57), "the thick-lips" (I.i.66), "an old black ram" (I.i.88), and "a Barbary horse" (I.i.113). Although Othello appears at the beginning of the second scene, we do not hear his name until well into Act I, scene iii (I.iii.48). Later, Othello's will be the last of the three ships to arrive at Cyprus in Act II, scene i; Othello will stand apart while Cassio and Iago supposedly discuss Desdemona in Act IV, scene i; and Othello will assume that Cassio is dead without being present when the fight takes place in Act V, scene i. Othello's status as an outsider may be the reason he is such easy prey for Iago.

Although Othello is a cultural and racial outsider in Venice, his skill as a soldier and leader is nevertheless valuable and necessary to the state, and he is an integral part of Venetian civic society. He is in great demand by the duke and senate, as evidenced by Cassio's comment that the senate "sent about three several quests" to look for Othello (I.ii.46). The Venetian government trusts Othello enough to put him in full martial and political command of Cyprus; indeed, in his dying speech, Othello reminds the Venetians of the "service" he has done their state (V.ii.348).

Those who consider Othello their social and civic peer, such as Desdemona and Brabanzio, nevertheless seem drawn to him because of his exotic qualities. Othello admits as much when he tells the duke about his friendship with Brabanzio. He says, "[Desdemona's] father loved me, oft invited me, / Still questioned me the story of my life / From year to year" (I.iii.127–129). Othello is also able to captivate his peers with his speech. The duke's reply to Othello's speech about how he wooed Desdemona with his tales of adventure is: "I think this tale would win my daughter too" (I.iii.170).

Othello sometimes makes a point of presenting himself as an outsider, whether because he recognizes his exotic appeal or because he is self-conscious of and defensive about his difference from other Venetians. For example, in spite of his obvious eloquence in Act I, scene iii, he protests, "Rude am I in my speech, / And little blessed with the soft phrase of peace" (I.iii.81–82). While Othello is never rude in his speech, he does allow his eloquence to suffer as he is put under increasing strain by Iago's plots. In the final moments of the play, Othello regains his composure and, once again, seduces both his onstage and offstage audiences with his words. The speech that precedes his suicide is a tale that could woo almost anyone. It is the tension between Othello's victimization at the hands of a foreign culture and his own willingness to torment himself that makes him a tragic figure rather than simply Iago's ridiculous puppet.

IAGO

Possibly the most heinous villain in Shakespeare, Iago is fascinating for his most terrible characteristic: his utter lack of convincing motivation for his actions. In the first scene, he claims to be angry at Othello for having passed him over for the position of lieutenant (I.i.7–32). At the end of Act I, scene iii, Iago says he thinks Othello may have slept with his wife, Emilia: "It is thought abroad that 'twixt my sheets / He has done my office" (I.iii.369–370). Iago mentions this suspicion again at the end of Act II, scene i, explaining that he lusts after Desdemona because he wants to get even with Othello "wife for wife" (II.i.286). None of these claims seems to adequately explain Iago's deep hatred of Othello, and Iago's lack of motivation—or his inability or unwillingness to express his true motivation—makes his actions all the more terrifying. He is willing to take revenge on anyone—Othello, Desdemona, Cassio, Roderigo, even Emilia—at the slightest provocation and enjoys the pain and damage he causes.

Iago is often funny, especially in his scenes with the foolish Roderigo, which serve as a showcase of Iago's manipulative abilities. He seems almost to wink at the audience as he revels in his own skill. As entertained spectators, we find ourselves on Iago's side when he is with Roderigo, but the interactions between the two also reveal a streak of cowardice in Iago—a cowardice that becomes manifest in the final scene, when Iago kills his own wife (V.ii.231–242).

Iago's murder of Emilia could also stem from the general hatred of women that he displays. Some readers have suggested that Iago's true, underlying motive for persecuting Othello is his homosexual love for the general. He certainly seems to take great pleasure in preventing Othello from enjoying marital happiness, and he expresses his love for Othello frequently and effusively.

It is Iago's talent for understanding and manipulating the desires of those around him that makes him both a powerful and a compelling figure. Iago is able to take the handkerchief from Emilia and know that he can deflect her questions; he is able to tell Othello of the handkerchief and know that Othello will not doubt him; he is able to tell the audience, "And what's he then that says I play the villain," and know that it will laugh as though he were a clown (II.iii.310). Though the most inveterate liar, Iago inspires all of the play's characters the trait that is most lethal to Othello: trust.

Desdemona

Desdemona is a more plausible, well-rounded figure than much criticism has given her credit for. Arguments that see Desdemona as stereotypically weak and submissive ignore the conviction and authority of her first speech ("My noble father, / I do perceive here a divided duty" [I.iii.179–180]) and her terse fury after Othello strikes her ("I have not deserved this" [IV.i.236]). Similarly, critics who argue that Desdemona's slightly bizarre bawdy jesting with Iago in Act II, scene i, is either an interpolation not written by Shakespeare or a mere vulgarity ignore the fact that Desdemona is young, sexual, and recently married. She later displays the same chiding, almost mischievous wit in Act III, scene iii, lines 61–84, when she attempts to persuade Othello to forgive Cassio.

Desdemona is at times a submissive character, most notably in her willingness to take credit for her own murder. In response to Emilia's question, "O, who hath done this deed?" Desdemona's final words are, "Nobody, I myself. Farewell. / Commend me to my kind lord. O, farewell" (V.ii.133–134). The play, then, depicts Desdemona contradictorily as a self-effacing, faithful wife and as a bold, independent personality. This contradiction may be intentional, meant to portray the way Desdemona herself feels after defending her choice of marriage to her father in Act I, scene iii, and then almost immediately being put in the position of defending her fidelity to her husband. She begins the play as a supremely independent person, but midway through she must struggle against all odds to convince Othello that she is not *too* independent. The manner in which Desdemona is murdered—smothered by a pillow in a bed covered in her wedding sheets—is symbolic: she is literally suffocated beneath the demands put on her fidelity. Since her first lines, Desdemona has seemed capable of meeting or even rising above those demands. In the end, Othello stifles the speech that made Desdemona so powerful.

Tragically, Desdemona is apparently aware of her imminent death. She, not Othello, asks Emilia to put her wedding sheets on the bed, and she asks Emilia to bury her in these sheets should she die first. The last time we see Desdemona before she awakens to find Othello standing over her with murder in his eyes, she sings a song she learned from her mother's maid: "She was in love; and he proved mad / And did forsake her. She had a song of willow. / . . . / And she died singing it. That song tonight / Will not go from my mind" (IV.iii.27–30). Like the audience, Desdemona seems able only to watch as her husband is driven insane with jealousy. Though she maintains to the end that she is "guiltless," Desdemona also forgives her husband (V.ii.133). Her forgiveness of Othello may help the audience to forgive him as well.

THEMES, MOTIFS & SYMBOLS

THEMES

Themes are the fundamental and often universal ideas explored in a literary work.

THE INCOMPATIBILITY OF MILITARY HEROISM & LOVE

Before and above all else, Othello is a soldier. From the earliest moments in the play, his career affects his married life. Asking "fit disposition" for his wife after being ordered to Cyprus (I.iii.234), Othello notes that "the tyrant custom . . . / Hath made the flinty and steel couch of war / My thrice-driven bed of down" (I.iii.227–229). While Desdemona is used to better "accommodation," she nevertheless accompanies her husband to Cyprus (I.iii.236). Moreover, she is unperturbed by the tempest or Turks that threatened their crossing, and genuinely curious rather than irate when she is roused from bed by the drunken brawl in Act II, scene iii. She is, indeed, Othello's "fair warrior," and he is happiest when he has her by his side in the midst of military conflict or business (II.i.179). The military also provides Othello with a means to gain acceptance in Venetian society. While the Venetians in the play are generally fearful of the prospect of Othello's social entrance into white society through his marriage to Desdemona, all Venetians respect and honor him as a soldier. Mercenary Moors were, in fact, commonplace at the time.

Othello predicates his success in love on his success as a soldier, wooing Desdemona with tales of his military travels and battles. Once the Turks are drowned—by natural rather than military might—Othello is left without anything to do: the last act of military administration we see him perform is the viewing of fortifications in the extremely short second scene of Act III. No longer having a means of proving his manhood or honor in a public setting such as the court or the battlefield, Othello begins to feel uneasy with his footing in a private setting, the bedroom. Iago capitalizes on this uneasiness, calling Othello's epileptic fit in Act IV, scene i, "[a] passion most unsuiting such a man." In other words, Iago is calling Othello unsoldierly. Iago also takes care to mention that Cassio, whom Othello believes to be his competitor, saw him in his emasculating trance (IV.i.75).

Desperate to cling to the security of his former identity as a soldier while his current identity as a lover crumbles, Othello begins to confuse the one with the other. His expression of his jealousy quickly devolves from the conventional—"Farewell the tranquil mind"—to the absurd:

> *Farewell the plum'd troops and the big wars*
> *That make ambition virtue! O, farewell,*
> *Farewell the neighing steed and the shrill trump,*
> *The spirit-stirring drum, th'ear piercing fife,*
> *The royal banner, and all quality,*
> *Pride, pomp, and circumstance of glorious war!"*
> *(III.iii.353–359)*

One might well say that Othello is saying farewell to the wrong things—he is entirely preoccupied with his identity as a soldier. But his way of thinking is somewhat justified by its seductiveness to the audience as well. Critics and audiences alike find comfort and nobility in Othello's final speech and the anecdote of the "malignant and . . . turbaned Turk" (V.ii.362), even though in that speech, as in his speech in Act III, scene iii, Othello depends on his identity as a soldier to glorify himself in the public's memory, and to try to make his audience forget his and Desdemona's disastrous marital experiment.

THE DANGER OF ISOLATION

The action of *Othello* moves from the metropolis of Venice to the island of Cyprus. Protected by military fortifications as well as by the forces of nature, Cyprus faces little threat from external forces. Once Othello, Iago, Desdemona, Emilia, and Roderigo have come to Cyprus, they have nothing to do but prey upon one another. Isolation enables many of the play's most important effects: Iago frequently speaks in soliloquies; Othello stands apart while Iago talks with Cassio in Act IV, scene i, and is left alone onstage with the bodies of Emilia and Desdemona for a few moments in Act V, scene ii; Roderigo seems attached to no one in the play except Iago. And, most prominently, Othello is visibly isolated from the other characters by his physical stature and the color of his skin. Iago is an expert at manipulating the distance between characters, isolating

THEMES

his victims so that they fall prey to their own obsessions. At the same time, Iago, of necessity always standing apart, falls prey to his own obsession with revenge. The characters *cannot* be islands, the play seems to say: self-isolation as an act of self-preservation leads ultimately to self-destruction. Such self-isolation leads to the deaths of Roderigo, Iago, Othello, and even Emilia.

MOTIFS

Motifs are recurring structures, contrasts, and literary devices that can help to develop and inform the text's major themes.

SIGHT AND BLINDNESS

When Desdemona asks to be allowed to accompany Othello to Cyprus, she says that she "saw Othello's visage in his mind, / And to his honours and his valiant parts / Did I my soul and fortunes consecrate" (I.iii. 250–252). Othello's blackness, his visible difference from everyone around him, is of little importance to Desdemona: she has the power to see him for what he is in a way that even Othello himself cannot. Desdemona's line is one of many references to different kinds of sight in the play. Earlier in Act I, scene iii, a senator suggests that the Turkish retreat to Rhodes is "a pageant / To keep us in false gaze" (I.iii.19–20). The beginning of Act II consists entirely of people staring out to sea, waiting to see the arrival of ships, friendly or otherwise. Othello, though he demands "ocular proof" (III.iii.365), is frequently convinced by things he does not see: he strips Cassio of his position as lieutenant based on the story Iago tells; he relies on Iago's story of seeing Cassio wipe his beard with Desdemona's handkerchief (III.iii.437–440); and he believes Cassio to be dead simply because he hears him scream. After Othello has killed himself in the final scene, Lodovico says to Iago, "Look on the tragic loading of this bed. / This is thy work. The object poisons sight. / Let it be hid" (V.ii.373–375). The action of the play depends heavily on characters *not* seeing things: Othello accuses his wife although he never sees her infidelity, and Emilia, although she watches Othello erupt into a rage about the missing handkerchief, does not figuratively "see" what her husband has done.

PLANTS

Iago is strangely preoccupied with plants. His speeches to Roderigo in particular make extensive and elaborate use of vegetable metaphors and conceits. Some examples are: "Our bodies are our gardens, to which our wills are gardeners; so that if we will plant nettles or sow lettuce, set hyssop and weed up thyme . . . the power and corrigible authority of this lies in our wills" (I.iii.317–322); "Though other things grow fair against the sun, / Yet fruits that blossom first will first be ripe" (II.iii.349–350); "And then, sir, would he gripe and wring my hand, / Cry 'O sweet creature!', then kiss me hard, / As if he plucked kisses up by the roots, / That grew upon my lips" (III.iii.425–428). The first of these examples best explains Iago's preoccupation with the plant metaphor and how it functions within the play. Characters in this play seem to be the product of certain inevitable, natural forces, which, if left unchecked, will grow wild. Iago understands these natural forces particularly well: he is, according to his own metaphor, a good "gardener," both of himself and of others.

Many of Iago's botanical references concern poison: "I'll pour this pestilence into his ear" (II.iii.330); "The Moor already changes with my poison. / Dangerous conceits are in their natures poisons, / . . . / . . . Not poppy nor mandragora / Nor all the drowsy syrups of the world / Shall ever medicine thee to that sweet sleep" (III.iii.329–336). Iago cultivates his "conceits" so that they become lethal poisons and then plants their seeds in the minds of others. The organic way in which Iago's plots consume the other characters and determine their behavior makes his conniving, human evil seem like a force of nature. That organic growth also indicates that the minds of the other characters are fertile ground for Iago's efforts.

ANIMALS

Iago calls Othello a "Barbary horse," an "old black ram," and also tells Brabanzio that his daughter and Othello are "making the beast with two backs" (I.i.117–118). In Act I, scene iii, Iago tells Roderigo, "Ere I would say I would drown myself for the love of a guinea-hen, I would change my humanity with a baboon" (I.iii.312–313). He then remarks that drowning is for "cats and blind puppies" (I.iii.330–331). Cassio laments that, when drunk, he is "by and by a fool, and presently a beast!" (II.iii.284–285). Othello tells Iago, "Exchange me for a goat / When I shall turn the business of my soul / To such exsufflicate and blowed surmises" (III.iii.184–186). He later says that "[a] horned man's a monster and a beast" (IV.i.59). Even Emilia, in the final scene, says that she will "play the swan, / And die in music" (V.ii.254–255). Like the repeated references to plants, these references to animals convey a sense that the laws of nature, rather than those of society, are the primary forces governing the characters in this play. When animal references are used with regard to Othello, as they frequently are, they reflect the racism both of characters in the play and of Shakespeare's contemporary audience. "Barbary horse" is a vulgarity particularly appropriate in the mouth of Iago, but even without having seen Othello, the Jacobean audience would have known from Iago's metaphor that he meant to connote a savage Moor.

HELL, DEMONS, AND MONSTERS
Iago tells Othello to beware of jealousy, the "green-eyed monster which doth mock/ The meat it feeds on" (III.iii.170–171). Likewise, Emilia describes jealousy as dangerously and uncannily self-generating, a "monster / Begot upon itself, born on itself" (III. iv.156–157). Imagery of hell and damnation also recurs throughout Othello, especially toward the end of the play, when Othello becomes preoccupied with the religious and moral judgment of Desdemona and himself. After he has learned the truth about Iago, Othello calls Iago a devil and a demon several times in Act V, scene ii. Othello's earlier allusion to "some monster in [his] thought" ironically refers to Iago (III.iii.111). Likewise, his vision of Desdemona's betrayal is "monstrous, monstrous!" (III.iii.431). Shortly before he kills himself, Othello wishes for eternal spiritual and physical torture in hell, crying out, "Whip me, ye devils, / . . . / . . . roast me in sulphur, / Wash me in steep-down gulfs of liquid fire!" (V.ii.284–287). The imagery of the monstrous and diabolical takes over where the imagery of animals can go no further, presenting the jealousy-crazed characters not simply as brutish, but as grotesque, deformed, and demonic.

SYMBOLS

Symbols are objects, characters, figures, and colors used to represent abstract ideas or concepts.

THE HANDKERCHIEF
The handkerchief symbolizes different things to different characters. Since the handkerchief was the first gift Desdemona received from Othello, she keeps it about her constantly as a symbol of Othello's

love. Iago manipulates the handkerchief so that Othello comes to see it as a symbol of Desdemona herself—her faith and chastity. By taking possession of it, he is able to convert it into evidence of her infidelity. But the handkerchief's importance to Iago and Desdemona derives from its importance to Othello himself. He tells Desdemona that it was woven by a 200-year-old sibyl, or female prophet, using silk from sacred worms and dye extracted from the hearts of mummified virgins. Othello claims that his mother used it to keep his father faithful to her, so, to him, the handkerchief represents marital fidelity. The pattern of strawberries (dyed with virgins' blood) on a white background strongly suggests the bloodstains left on the sheets on a virgin's wedding night, so the handkerchief implicitly suggests a guarantee of virginity as well as fidelity.

The Song "Willow"

As she prepares for bed in Act V, Desdemona sings a song about a woman who is betrayed by her lover. She was taught the song by her mother's maid, Barbary, who suffered a misfortune similar to that of the woman in the song; she even died singing "Willow." The song's lyrics suggest that both men and women are unfaithful to one another. To Desdemona, the song seems to represent a melancholy and resigned acceptance of her alienation from Othello's affections, and singing it leads her to question Emilia about the nature and practice of infidelity.

SYMBOLS

SUMMARY & ANALYSIS

ACT I, SCENES I–II

SUMMARY: ACT I, SCENE I

> *In following him I follow but myself;*
> *Heaven is my judge, not I for love and duty,*
> *But seeming so for my peculiar end.*
>
> *(See* QUOTATIONS, *p. 55)*

Othello begins on a street in Venice, in the midst of an argument between Roderigo and Iago. The rich Roderigo has been paying Iago to help him in his suit to Desdemona, but he has seen no progress, and he has just learned that Desdemona has married Othello, a general whom Iago serves as ensign. Iago reassures Roderigo that he hates Othello. Chief among Iago's reasons for this hatred is Othello's recent promotion of Michael Cassio to the post of lieutenant. In spite of Iago's service in battle and the recommendation of three "great ones" of the city, Othello chose to give the position to a man with no experience leading men in battle. As he waits for an opportunity to further his own self-interest, Iago only pretends to serve Othello.

Iago advises Roderigo to spoil some of Othello's pleasure in his marriage by rousing Desdemona's family against the general. The two men come to the street outside the house of Desdemona's father, Brabanzio, and cry out that he has been robbed by "thieves." Brabanzio, who is a Venetian senator, comes to the window. At first, he doesn't believe what he hears, because he has told Roderigo to stay away from his daughter before and thinks Roderigo is merely scheming once again in order to see Desdemona. Iago speaks in inflammatory terms, vulgarly telling the senator that his daughter and Othello are having sex by saying that they are "making the beast with two backs" (I.i.118). Brabanzio begins to take what he hears seriously and decides to search for his daughter. Seeing the success of his plan, Iago leaves Roderigo alone and goes to attend on Othello. Like Brabanzio, Othello has no idea of Iago's role in Roderigo's accusations. As Iago departs, Brabanzio comes out of his house, furious that his daughter has left him. Declaring that his daughter has been stolen from him by magic "charms," Brabanzio and his men follow Roderigo to Othello.

SUMMARY: ACT I, SCENE II

Iago arrives at Othello's lodgings, where he warns the general that Brabanzio will not hesitate to attempt to force a divorce between Othello and Desdemona. Othello sees a party of men approaching, and Iago, thinking that Brabanzio and his followers have arrived, counsels Othello to retreat indoors. Othello stands his ground, but the party turns out to be Cassio and officers from the Venetian court. They bring Othello the message that he is wanted by the duke of Venice about a matter concerning Cyprus, an island in the Mediterranean Sea controlled by Venice. As Cassio and his men prepare to leave, Iago mentions that Othello is married, but before he can say any more, Brabanzio, Roderigo, and Brabanzio's men arrive to accost Othello. Brabanzio orders his men to attack and subdue Othello. A struggle between Brabanzio's and Othello's followers seems imminent, but Othello brings the confrontation to a halt by calmly and authoritatively telling both sides to put up their swords. Hearing that the duke has summoned Othello to the court, Brabanzio decides to bring his cause before the duke himself.

ANALYSIS: ACT I, SCENES I–II

The action of the first scene heightens the audience's anticipation of Othello's first appearance. We learn Iago's name in the second line of the play and Roderigo's soon afterward, but Othello is not once mentioned by his name. Rather, he is ambiguously referred to as "he" and "him." He is also called "the Moor" (I.i.57), "the thick-lips" (I.i.66), and "a Barbary horse" (I.i.113)—all names signifying that he is dark-skinned.

Iago plays on the senator's fears, making him imagine a barbarous and threatening Moor, or native of Africa, whose bestial sexual appetite has turned him into a thief and a rapist. Knowing nothing of Othello, one would expect that the audience, too, would be seduced by Iago's portrait of the general, but several factors keep us from believing him. In the first place, Roderigo is clearly a pathetic and jealous character. He adores Desdemona, but she has married Othello and seems unaware of Roderigo's existence. Roderigo doesn't even have the ability to woo Desdemona on his own: he has already appealed to Brabanzio for Desdemona's hand, and when that fails, he turns to Iago for help. Rich and inexperienced, Roderigo naïvely gives his money to Iago in exchange for vague but unfulfilled promises of amorous success.

The fact that Iago immediately paints himself as the villain also prepares us to be sympathetic to Othello. Iago explains to Roderigo that he has no respect for Othello beyond what he has to show to further his own revenge: "I follow him to serve my turn upon him" (I.i.42). Iago explicitly delights in his villainy, always tipping the audience off about his plotting. In these first two scenes, Iago tells Roderigo to shout beneath Brabanzio's window and predicts exactly what will happen when they do so. Once Brabanzio has been roused, Iago also tells Roderigo where he can meet Othello. Because of the dramatic irony Iago establishes, the audience is forced into a position of feeling intimately connected with Iago's villainy.

In many ways, Iago is the driving force behind the plot, a playwright of sorts whose machinations inspire the action of the play. His self-conscious falseness is highly theatrical, calculated to shock the audience. Iago is a classic two-faced villain, a type of character known in Shakespeare's time as a "Machiavel"—a villain who, adhering all too literally to the teachings of the political philosopher Machiavelli, lets nothing stand in his way in his quest for power. He is also reminiscent of the stock character of Vice from medieval morality plays, who also announces to the audience his diabolical schemes.

After having been prepared for a passionate and possibly violent personage in Othello, the quiet calm of Othello's character—his dismissal of Roderigo's alleged insult and his skillful avoidance of conflict—is surprising. In fact, far from presenting Othello as a savage barbarian, Shakespeare implicitly compares him to Christ. The moment when Brabanzio and his men arrive with swords and torches, tipped off to Othello's whereabouts by Othello's disloyal friend, vividly echoes John 18:1–11. In that Gospel, Christ and his followers are met by officers carrying swords and torches. The officers were informed of Christ's whereabouts by Judas, who pretends to side with Christ in the ensuing confrontation. When Othello averts the violence that seems imminent with a single sentence, "Keep up your bright swords, for the dew will rust 'em" (I.ii.60), he echoes Christ's command to Peter, "Put up thy sword into the sheath" (John 18:11). However, whereas Christ's calm restraint is due to his resigned acceptance of his fate, Othello's is due to his sense of his own authority.

Brabanzio twice accuses Othello of using magic to seduce his daughter (in I.i.172–173 and I.ii.73–80), and he repeats the same charge a third time in front of the duke in Act I, scene iii. Even though Shakespeare's audience would have considered elopement with a nobleman's daughter to be a serious, possibly imprisonable offense, Brabanzio insists that he wants to arrest and prosecute Othello specifically for the crime of witchcraft, not for eloping with his daughter without his consent. Brabanzio's racism is clear—he claims that he simply cannot believe that Desdemona would be attracted to the Moor unless her reason and senses were blinded. Yet, it is possible that Brabanzio is not being sincere. He may feel that he needs to accuse Othello of a crime more serious than elopement because he knows the duke will overlook Othello's infraction otherwise.

Act I, scene iii

Summary

> But here's my husband,
> And so much duty as my mother showed
> To you, preferring you before her father,
> So much I challenge that I may profess
> Due to the Moor my lord.
>
> (See QUOTATIONS, p. 56)

The duke's meeting with his senators about the imminent Turkish invasion of Cyprus takes an unexpected turn when a sailor arrives and announces that the Turks seem to have turned toward Rhodes, another island controlled by Venice. One of the senators guesses that the Turks' change of course is intended to mislead the Venetians, because Cyprus is more important to the Turks and far more vulnerable than Rhodes. This guess proves to be correct, as another messenger arrives to report that the Turks have joined with more forces and are heading back toward Cyprus.

This military meeting is interrupted by the arrival of Brabanzio, Othello, Cassio, Iago, Roderigo, and officers. Brabanzio demands that all state business be put aside to address his own grievance—his daughter has been stolen from him by spells and potions purchased from charlatans. The duke is initially eager to take Brabanzio's side, but he becomes more skeptical when he learns that Othello is the man accused. The duke gives Othello the chance to speak for himself. Othello admits that he married Desdemona, but he denies having used magic to woo her and claims that Desdemona will support his story. He explains that Brabanzio frequently invited him to his house and questioned him about his remarkable life story, full of harrowing battles, travels outside the civilized world, and dramatic reversals of fortune. Desdemona overheard parts of the story and found a convenient time to ask Othello to retell it to her. Desdemona was moved to love Othello by his story.

The duke is persuaded by Othello's tale, dismissing Brabanzio's claim by remarking that the story probably would win his own daughter. Desdemona enters, and Brabanzio asks her to tell those present to whom she owes the most obedience. Brabanzio clearly expects her to say her father. Desdemona, however, confirms that she married Othello of her own free will and that, like her own mother before her, she must shift her primary loyalty from father to husband. Brabanzio reluctantly resigns himself to her decision and allows the court to return to state affairs.

The duke decides that Othello must go to Cyprus to defend the island from the Turks. Othello is willing and ready to go, and he asks that appropriate accommodations be provided for his wife. The duke suggests that she stay with her father, but neither Desdemona nor Brabanzio nor Othello will accept this, and Desdemona asks to be allowed to go with Othello. The couple then leaves to prepare for the night's voyage.

The stage is cleared, leaving only Roderigo and Iago. Once again, Roderigo feels that his hopes of winning Desdemona have been dashed, but Iago insists that all will be well. Iago mocks Roderigo for threatening to drown himself, and Roderigo protests that he can't help being tormented by love. Iago contradicts him, asserting that people can choose at will what they want to be. "Put but money in thy purse," Iago tells Roderigo repeatedly in the paragraph that spans lines 329–351, urging him to follow him to Cyprus. Iago promises to work everything out from there. When Roderigo leaves, Iago delivers his first soliloquy, declaring his hatred for Othello and his suspicion that Othello has slept with his wife, Emilia. He lays out his plan to cheat Roderigo out of his money, to convince Othello that Cassio has slept with Desdemona, and to use Othello's honest and unsuspecting nature to bring him to his demise.

ANALYSIS

The war between the Turks and Venetians will not prove to be a major part of the play. However, the Turks' "feint"—in which they pretend to sail toward Rhodes to mislead the Venetians into thinking that they will not attack Cyprus—has a symbolic significance. Throughout the play, deception is one of Iago's major weapons, and his attacks on other characters are particularly devastating because his enemies don't know that he is attacking them.

Othello is both an outsider and an insider in Venetian society. His race, physical appearance, and remarkable life history set him apart from the other Venetians, and inspire Brabanzio's fears that Othello is some sort of witch doctor. At the same time, the duke and other characters treat him as an essential part of the Venetian state. When Othello and the others enter, the duke gets straight to business, telling Othello that they must immediately employ him against the Ottoman Turks. Only after delivering these two lines does the duke notice Brabanzio, and, even then, he acknowledges him in a rather demeaning fashion, saying, "I did not see you. Welcome, gentle signor" (I.iii.50). Brabanzio's lengthy calls for justice are met only with the duke's desire to hear more from Othello, and once Othello has delivered his long and beautiful speech about wooing Desdemona, the duke feels the subject is closed. As both a physical and a political presence, Othello overshadows Brabanzio.

Shakespeare fleshed out the fantastic details of Othello's past life by drawing on a number of ancient and Renaissance travel writers. Othello clearly attaches great importance to the image of himself as a unique and heroic figure, and it is also important to him that he have a remarkable life story worthy of repeated telling. Not only does he claim that Desdemona fell in love with him because of his story, he says that he fell in love with her because of her reaction to his story. Desdemona confirms or validates something about Othello's self-image, which may suggest why her faithfulness is of such all-consuming importance to him.

Desdemona herself appears remarkably forward and aggressive in Othello's account, particularly in relation to Renaissance expectations of female behavior. She "devour[s] up" his discourse with a "greedy ear," and is the first of the two to hint at the possibility of their loving one another (I.iii.148–149). Exactly how forward we should imagine Desdemona to be is somewhat uncertain. Modern texts of the play are based upon one of two early editions of Shakespeare's plays, the Quarto edition and the Folio edition. (Quarto and Folio refer to two different sizes of books.) In the Quarto, Othello says, "My story being done, / She gave me for my pains a world of sighs," whereas in the Folio, he says, "She gave me for my pains a world of kisses" (I.iii.157–158). In both editions, Othello is ambiguous about whether he or Desdemona played the more active role in the courtship, which could mean that he is somewhat uncomfortable—either embarrassed or upset—with Desdemona's aggressive pursuit of him. In Act I, scene ii, lines 149–154, for instance, he says that he observed that Desdemona wanted him to retell his tale, so he found a way to get her to ask him to tell it, and then he consented. This seems an unnecessarily complicated way of describing what happened, and suggests either that Othello was uncertain which of them played the leading role or that he wants to insist that his own role was more active than it actually was.

When Desdemona finally enters and speaks for herself, she does indeed seem outspoken and assertive, as well as generous and devoted. In her speech about her "divided duty" as a wife and a daughter, Desdemona shows herself to be poised and intelligent, as capable of loving as of being loved, and able to weigh her competing loyalties respectfully and judiciously (I.iii.180). In arguing for her right to accompany Othello to Cyprus, she insists upon the "violence" and unconventionality of her attachment to Othello (I.iii.248–249). In declaring "I did love the Moor to live with him," she frankly insists on the sexual nature of her love (I.iii.248). She is saying that she isn't content to marvel at Othello's stories; she wants to share his bed. As the plot progresses, Desdemona's sexual aggressiveness will upset Othello more and more. In explaining her love for Othello, she states that she "saw Othello's visage in his mind," which might mean either that she saw a different face inside him than the one the rest of the world sees, or "I saw him as he sees himself," supporting the idea that she validates or upholds Othello's sense of self.

ACT II, SCENES I–II

SUMMARY: ACT II, SCENE I
On the shores of Cyprus, Montano, the island's governor, watches a storm with two gentlemen. Just as Montano says that the Turkish fleet of ships could not survive the storm, a third gentlemen comes to confirm his prediction: as his ship traveled from Venice, Cassio witnessed that the Turks lost most of their fleet in the tempest. It

is still uncertain whether Othello's ship has been able to survive the storm. Hope lifts as voices offstage announce the sighting of a sail offshore, but the new ship turns out to be carrying Iago, Emilia, Desdemona, and Roderigo. Desdemona disembarks, and no sooner does Cassio tell her that Othello has yet to arrive than a friendly shot announces the arrival of a third ship. While the company waits for the ship, Cassio and Desdemona tease Emilia about being a chatterbox, but Iago quickly takes the opportunity to criticize women in general as deceptive and hypocritical, saying they are lazy in all matters except sex: "You rise to play and go to bed to work" (II.i.118). Desdemona plays along, laughing as Iago belittles women, whether beautiful or ugly, intelligent or stupid, as equally despicable. Cassio takes Desdemona away to speak with her privately about Othello's arrival. Iago notices that Cassio takes Desdemona's hand as he talks to her, and, in an aside, Iago plots to use Cassio's hand-holding to frame him so that he loses his newly gained promotion to lieutenant. "With as little a web as this I will ensnare as great a fly as Cassio," he asserts (II.i.169).

Othello arrives safely and greets Desdemona, expressing his devotion to her and giving her a kiss. He then thanks the Cypriots for their welcome and hospitality, and orders Iago to unload the ship. All but Roderigo and Iago head to the castle to celebrate the drowning of the Turks. Iago tells the despondent Roderigo that Desdemona will soon grow tired of being with Othello and will long for a more well-mannered and handsome man. But, Iago continues, the obvious first choice for Desdemona will be Cassio, whom Iago characterizes over and over again as a "knave" (II.i.231–239). Roderigo tries to argue that Cassio was merely being polite by taking Desdemona's hand, but Iago convinces him of Cassio's ill intentions and convinces Roderigo to start a quarrel with Cassio that evening. He posits that the uproar the quarrel will cause in the still tense city will make Cassio fall out of favor with Othello. Left alone onstage again, Iago explains his actions to the audience in a soliloquy. He secretly lusts after Desdemona, partially because he suspects that Othello has slept with Emilia, and he wants to get even with the Moor "wife for wife" (II.i.286). But, Iago continues, if he is unable to get his revenge by sleeping with Desdemona, Roderigo's accusation of Cassio will make Othello suspect his lieutenant of sleeping with his wife and torture Othello to madness.

SUMMARY: ACT II, SCENE II

A herald announces that Othello plans revelry for the evening in celebration of Cyprus's safety from the Turks, and also in celebration of his marriage to Desdemona.

ANALYSIS: ACT II, SCENES I–II

Like Act I, scene ii, the first scene of Act II begins with emphasis on the limitations of sight. "What from the cape can you discern at sea?" Montano asks, and the gentleman replies, "Nothing at all. It is a high-wrought flood" (II.i.1–2). The emphasis on the limitations of physical sight in a tempest foreshadows what will, after Act III, become Othello's metaphorical blindness, caused by his passion and rage. Similarly, once the physical threat that the Turks pose has been eliminated, the more psychological, less tangible threat posed by inner demons assumes dramatic precedence.

The play extinguishes the external threat with almost ridiculous speed. The line "News, lads! Our wars are done," is all that is needed to dismiss the plot involving the Turks (II.i.20). It is as though one kind of play ends at the end of Act II, scene ii, and another begins: what seemed to be a political tragedy becomes a domestic tragedy. Whereas the action of the play began on the streets of Venice and proceeded to the court and then to the beaches of Cyprus, it now moves to the passageways of Othello's residence on the island and ultimately ends in his bedchamber. The effect is almost cinematic—like a long and gradual close-up that restricts the visible space around the tragic hero, emphasizing his metaphorical blindness and symbolizing his imprisonment in his own jealous fantasies. This ever-tightening focus has led many readers to characterize the play as "claustrophobic."

The banter between Iago and Desdemona creates a nervous, uncomfortable atmosphere, in part because their levity is inappropriate, given that Othello's ship remains missing. The rhyming couplets in which Iago expresses his misogynistic insults lend them an eerie, alienating quality, and Desdemona's active encouragement of Iago is somewhat puzzling. Once again, Desdemona establishes herself as an outspoken and independent woman—she does not depend upon her husband's presence either socially or intellectually. However, Desdemona does not suggest that she has any interest in cheating on her husband. Iago himself tells us that he will make a mountain out of the molehill represented by Cassio's holding of Desdemona's hand.

Although Iago verbally abuses women in this scene—presumably because it is safe for him to do so—his real resentment seems to be against those characters who have a higher social class than he has, including Cassio and Desdemona. Iago resents Cassio for being promoted ahead of him, and Cassio's promotion is likely due to his higher class status. At the beginning of the play, Iago argued that he ought to have been promoted based upon his worth as a soldier, and he expressed bitterness that "[p]referment goes by letter and affection, / And not by old gradation" (I.i.35–36). In Act II, scene i, Cassio contributes to Iago's anger by taunting the ensign about his inferior status: "Let it not gall your patience, good Iago, / That I extend my manners. 'Tis my breeding / That gives me this bold show of courtesy" (II.i.100–102). Not long afterward, Iago makes fun of Roderigo for being "base" (meaning lower class), even though the play does not indicate that Roderigo is, in fact, of lower status than Iago (II.i.212).

In the soliloquy that concludes Act II, scene i, Iago once again explains quite clearly what he intends to do, despite his comment that his plan is "yet confused" (II.i.298). At the same time, his statements about what motivates him are hazy and confusing. Is he motivated by lust for Desdemona, envy of Cassio, or jealousy over his wife's supposed affair with Othello? He even throws in a bizarre parenthetical suspicion that Cassio might also have slept with his wife (II.i.294). It is as though Iago mocks the audience for attempting to determine his motives; he treats the audience as he does Othello and Roderigo, leading his listeners "by th' nose / As asses are [led]" (I.iii.383–384). For each of Iago's actions, he creates a momentary and unimportant justification.

ACT II, SCENE III

SUMMARY

Othello leaves Cassio on guard during the revels, reminding him to practice self-restraint during the celebration. Othello and Desdemona leave to consummate their marriage. Once Othello is gone, Iago enters and joins Cassio on guard. He tells Cassio that he suspects Desdemona to be a temptress, but Cassio maintains that she is modest. Then, despite Cassio's protestations, Iago persuades Cassio to take a drink and to invite some revelers to join them.

Once Cassio leaves to fetch the revelers, Iago tells the audience his plan: Roderigo and three other Cypriots, all of whom are drunk, will join Iago and Cassio on guard duty. Amidst all the drunkards, Iago will lead Cassio into committing an action that will disgrace him. Cassio returns, already drinking, with Montano and his attendants. It is not long before he becomes intoxicated and wanders offstage, assuring his friends that he isn't drunk. Once Cassio leaves, Iago tells Montano that while Cassio is a wonderful soldier, he fears that Cassio may have too much responsibility for someone with such a serious drinking problem. Roderigo enters, and Iago points him in Cassio's direction. As Montano continues to suggest that something be said to Othello of Cassio's drinking problem, Cassio chases Roderigo across the stage, threatening to beat him. Montano steps in to prevent the fight and is attacked by Cassio. Iago orders Roderigo to leave and "cry a mutiny" (II.iii.140). As Montano and others attempt to hold Cassio down, Cassio stabs Montano. An alarm bell is rung, and Othello arrives with armed attendants.

Immediately taking control of the situation, Othello demands to know what happened, but both Iago and Cassio claim to have forgotten how the struggle began. Montano insists that he is in too much pain to speak and insists that Iago tell the story. At first Iago feigns reluctance to incriminate Cassio, emphasizing the fact that he was chasing after Roderigo (to whom Iago does not refer by name) when the fight between Cassio and Montano began, and suggesting that the unknown man must have done something to upset Cassio. Othello falls into Iago's trap, stating that he can tell that Iago softened the story out of honest affection for Cassio. Othello dismisses Cassio from his service.

Desdemona has been awakened by the commotion, and Othello leads her back to bed, saying that he will look to Montano's wound. Iago and Cassio remain behind, and Cassio laments the permanent damage now done to his reputation by a quarrel whose cause he cannot even remember. Iago suggests that Cassio appeal to Desdemona, because she commands Othello's attention and goodwill. Iago argues that Desdemona's kindheartedness will prompt her to help Cassio if Cassio entreats her, and that she will persuade Othello to give Cassio back his lieutenantship.

When Cassio leaves, Iago jokes about the irony of the fact that his so-called villainy involves counseling Cassio to a course of action that would actually help him. He repeats what he told Cassio about Desdemona's generosity and Othello's devotion to her. However, as Iago reminds the audience, he does the most evil when he seems to do good. Now that Cassio will be spending time with Desdemona,

Iago will find it all the easier to convince Othello that Desdemona is having an affair with Cassio, thus turning Desdemona's virtue to "pitch" (II.iii.234).

Roderigo enters, upset that he has been beaten and angry because Iago has taken all his money and left Roderigo nothing to show for it. Iago counsels him to be patient and not to return to Venice, reminding him that they have to work by their wits. He assures Roderigo that everything is going according to plan. After telling Roderigo to go, Iago finishes telling the audience the plot that is to come: he will convince Emilia to speak to Desdemona on Cassio's behalf, and he will arrange for Othello to witness Cassio's suit to Desdemona.

Analysis

The brawl in Act II, scene iii, foreshadows Act V, scene i, where Cassio is stabbed and Roderigo is killed in a commotion outside a brothel. Cassio's comments about his own drinking, along with Othello's warning to Cassio at the scene's opening, show that Cassio is predisposed to licentiousness, and Iago, always skillful at manipulating human frailties, capitalizes on Cassio's tendency to get himself into trouble in situations involving pleasures of the flesh. Further evidence of Iago's skill as a manipulator is his ability to make Roderigo virtually invisible in the scene. Once Cassio has chased him across the stage and stabbed Montano, no one gives a second thought to the man who may or may not have begun the fight. No one seems to have any idea who Roderigo is (even though he is always onstage, even in the court scene of Act I, scene iii), and Cassio cannot even remember what they quarreled about.

When, in the middle of the commotion of Act II, scene iii, a sleepy Desdemona enters and asks, "What's the matter, dear?" Othello is the consummate gentle husband: "All's well now, sweeting. / Come away to bed" (II.iii.235–237). Othello and Desdemona's marriage appears to be sheltered from outside forces. Othello has just stopped the brawl, punished Cassio, and taken care of Montano; he is now ready to return home with his wife. By way of apology to his new bride for the inconveniences of her new way of life, he says, "Come Desdemona. 'Tis the soldiers' life / To have their balmy slumbers waked with strife" (II.iii.241–242). This is the last time we will see the couple so happy. The next time Othello sends Desdemona to bed is at the beginning of Act IV, scene ii, when he is preparing to kill her.

At the beginning of the scene, Othello says to Desdemona: "Come, my dear love, / The purchase made, the fruits are to ensue. / The profit's yet to come 'tween me and you" (II.iii.8–10). This comment seems to indicate that the couple has not yet consummated their marriage—the "purchase" is the wedding, and the "fruits" are the sex. Alternatively, Othello could be saying that he and Desdemona *have* consummated their marriage—"the purchase" is Desdemona's virginity, and "the fruits" could be pleasant sex as opposed to the pain of the consummation.

Iago has now interrupted Othello's conjugal efforts twice. Iago's speeches clearly show him to be obsessed with sex. For instance, when Othello bursts onto the scene and demands to know what is going on, Iago answers by comparing the party to a bride and groom undressing for bed (II.iii.163–165). He seems to take great pleasure in preventing Othello from enjoying marital happiness. Some readers have suggested that Iago's true, underlying motive for persecuting Othello is his homosexual love for the general. In addition to disrupting Othello's marriage, he expresses his love for Othello frequently and effusively, and he seems to hate women in general.

As Othello breaks up the brawl, he demands, "Are we turned Turks, and to ourselves do that / Which heaven hath forbid the Ottomites?" (II.iii.153–54). Othello, himself an "other" on the inside of Venetian society, and one who will ultimately upset the order of that society, calls attention to the potential for all external threats to become internal. It is that potential which Iago will continually exploit.

Act III, scenes i–iii

Summary: Act III, scene i

In an effort to win Othello's good graces, Cassio sends musicians to play music beneath the general's window. Othello sends his servant, a clown, or peasant, to tell the musicians to go away. Cassio asks the clown to entreat Emilia to come speak with him, so that he can ask her for access to Desdemona. When the clown leaves, Iago enters and tells Cassio that he will send for Emilia straightaway and figure out a way to take Othello aside so that Cassio and Desdemona can confer privately. After Iago exits, Emilia enters and tells Cassio that Othello and Desdemona have been discussing his case. Desdemona has pleaded for Cassio, but Othello worries that Montano's influence and popularity in Cyprus would make Cassio's reappointment impractical, no matter how much Othello cares for his former lieu-tenant. Emilia allows Cassio to come in and tells him to wait for Desdemona.

SUMMARY: ACT III, SCENE II

Iago, Othello, and a gentleman walk together at the citadel. Othello gives Iago some letters to deliver and decides to take a look at the town's fortification.

SUMMARY: ACT III, SCENE III

> *This was her first remembrance from the Moor,*
> *My wayward husband hath a hundred times*
> *Wooed me to steal it, but she so loves the token. . . .*
>
> *(See* QUOTATIONS, *p. 58)*

Desdemona, Cassio, and Emilia enter mid-conversation. Desdemo-na has just vowed to do everything she can on Cassio's behalf when Othello and Iago enter. Cassio quickly departs, protesting to Desde-mona that he feels too uneasy to do himself any good. Othello asks whether it was Cassio he saw leaving the room, and Iago responds that surely Cassio would not behave like a guilty man at Othello's approach.

Desdemona entreats Othello to forgive Cassio and reinstate him as lieutenant. Othello assures her that he will speak to Cassio, but he answers evasively when she tries to set a meeting time. She criticizes Othello for responding to her request so grudgingly and hesitantly, and he tells her that he will deny her nothing but wishes to be left to himself for a little while.

Alone with Othello, Iago begins his insinuations of an affair be-tween Cassio and Desdemona by reminding Othello that Cassio served as Othello and Desdemona's go-between during their court-ship. Othello asks Iago whether he believes Cassio to be honest, and Iago feigns reluctance to answer. Iago plants in Othello's mind thoughts of adultery, cuckoldry, and hypocrisy, until Othello screams at the ensign to speak his mind. Iago suggests that Othello observe his wife closely when she is with Cassio.

Othello tells Iago to have Emilia watch Desdemona when she is with Cassio. Iago appears to retreat from his accusations and sug-gests that Othello leave the matter alone. But he has already made his point. By himself, Othello muses that his wife no longer loves him, probably because he is too old for her, because he is black, and because he doesn't have the manners of a courtier. "She's gone," he laments (III.iii.271).

Desdemona and Emilia enter to inform Othello that he is expected at dinner. Othello says that he has a pain in his forehead, and Desdemona offers to bind his head with her handkerchief. Othello pushes her handkerchief away, telling her that it is too small. The handkerchief drops to the floor, where it remains as Othello and Desdemona exit. Emilia, staying behind, picks up the handkerchief, remarking that her husband has asked her to steal it at least a hundred times. Iago enters, and Emilia teases him with the promise of a surprise. He is ecstatic when she gives it to him, and sends her away.

As Iago gleefully plots to plant the handkerchief in Cassio's room, Othello enters and flies into a rage at him. Othello declares that his soul is in torment, and that it would be better to be deceived completely than to suspect without proof. He demands that Iago bring him visual evidence that Desdemona is a whore. Iago protests that it would be impossible to actually witness Desdemona and Cassio having sex, even if the two were as lustful as animals. He promises that he can provide circumstantial evidence, however. First, he tells Othello that while Cassio and Iago were sharing a bed, Cassio called out Desdemona's name in his sleep, wrung Iago's hand, kissed him hard on the lips, and threw his leg over Iago's thigh. This story enrages Othello, and Iago reminds him that it was only Cassio's dream. Iago then claims to have witnessed Cassio wiping his beard with the handkerchief Othello gave Desdemona as her first gift. Furious, Othello cries out for blood. He kneels and vows to heaven that he will take his revenge on Desdemona and Cassio, and Iago kneels with him, vowing to help execute his master's vengeance. Othello promotes Iago to lieutenant.

ANALYSIS: ACT III, SCENES I–III

> *Haply for I am black,*
> *And have not those soft parts of conversation*
> *That chamberers have; or for I am declined*
> *Into the vale of years—yet that's not much—*
> *She's gone.*
>
> *(See* QUOTATIONS, *p. 57)*

The timing of events is very important in Act III. Iago anticipates and manipulates the other characters so skillfully that they seem to be acting simultaneously of their own free will and as Iago's puppets.

(sidebar) SUMMARY & ANALYSIS

For example, it takes only the slightest prompting on Iago's part to put Othello into the proper frame of mind to be consumed by jealousy—Iago exploits Cassio's discomfort upon seeing Othello by interpreting it as a sign of guilt. Iago's interpretation of Cassio's exit, combined with Desdemona's vigorous advocating on Cassio's behalf, creates suspicion in Othello's mind even before Iago prompts Othello. Othello manifests his confusion about his wife by telling her that he wishes to be left alone, and by spurning her offer of help when he tells her that he feels unwell.

When Desdemona advocates on Cassio's behalf, she initiates the first real onstage conversation she has had with her husband throughout the play. She also displays her strong, generous, and independent personality. In addition to his burgeoning suspicion, Othello's moodiness may also result from his dislike of Desdemona herself. Only once Desdemona has left does Othello recover somewhat: "Excellent wretch!" he says affectionately. "Perdition catch my soul / But I do love thee, and when I love thee not, / Chaos is come again" (III.iii.91–93). Othello seems far more comfortable expressing his love for Desdemona when she is absent. Perhaps this is because her presence makes him conscious of her claim upon him and of his obligation to honor her requests, or perhaps this is because he is more in love with some idea or image of Desdemona than he is with Desdemona herself. The lines just quoted indicate how much his image of her means to him: if he stops loving her, the entire universe stops making sense for him, and the world is reduced to "Chaos."

Given how much is at stake for Othello in his idea of Desdemona, it is remarkable how he becomes completely consumed by jealousy in such a short time. Moreover, it takes very little evidence to convince him of her unfaithfulness. All Iago has to do to Othello is make him doubt Desdemona, and jealousy spreads like a virus until he rejects her absolutely. Notably, Iago, too, has no evidence that Othello has slept with Emilia, but the suspicion or doubt seems to have been sufficient to make him spurn Emilia and persecute Othello. As Othello says, "[T]o be once in doubt / Is once to be resolved" (III.iii.183–184).

Othello soon learns, however, that to be once in doubt is to be *never* resolved. He leaves the stage briefly after the episode in which he rejects Desdemona's handkerchief, at which point he seems resolved that his wife no longer loves him. A mere forty lines later, he returns, and all he can think about is garnering proof of her infidelity. The paradox in Othello's situation is that there are few things—the nature of friends, enemies, and wives included—that a human being can know with certainty. Most relationships must be accepted based on faith or trust, a quality that Othello is unwilling to extend to his own wife. All Iago really has to do to provoke Othello is to remind him that he doesn't know for certain what his wife is doing or feeling. Iago's advice that Othello "[l]ook to [his] wife. Observe her well. . . ." appears harmless at first, until one considers how out of the ordinary it is for a husband to "observe" his wife as if she were a specimen under a microscope (III. iii.201). For a man to treat his wife as a problem to be solved or a thing to be known, rather than as a person with a claim upon him, is simply incompatible with the day-to-day business of being married.Othello's rejection of his wife's offering of physical solace (via the handkerchief), and his termination of the exchange in which Desdemona argues for Cassio, thereby asserting a marital right, clearly demonstrate this incompatibility.

Ironically, Iago doesn't have to prove his own fidelity to Othello for Othello to take everything Iago suggests on faith. On the contrary, Othello actually infers that Iago holds back more damning knowledge of Desdemona's offenses out of his great love for Othello. Again and again, Iago insists that he speaks out only because of this love. His claim, "My lord, you know I love you" (III.iii.121) even echoes Peter's insistent words to Christ, "Lord, thou knowest that I love thee" (John 21:15–17).

Othello's rejection of Desdemona's offer of her handkerchief is an emphatic rejection of Desdemona herself. He tells her he has a pain "upon" his forehead and dismisses her handkerchief as "too little" to bind his head with, implying that invisible horns are growing out of his head. Horns are the traditional symbol of the cuckold, a husband whose wife is unfaithful to him. Othello's indirect allusion to these horns suggests that the thought of being a cuckold causes him pain but that he is not willing to confront his wife directly with his suspicions.

The end of Act III, scene iii, is the climax of *Othello*. Convinced of his wife's corruption, Othello makes a sacred oath never to change his mind about her or to soften his feelings toward her until he enacts a violent revenge. At this point, Othello is fixed in his course, and the disastrous ending of the play is unavoidable. Othello engages Iago in a perverse marriage ceremony, in which each kneels and solemnly pledges to the other to take vengeance on Desdemona and Cassio. Just as the play replaces the security of peace with the anxiety of domestic strife, Othello replaces the security of his marriage with the hateful paranoia of an alliance with Iago. Iago's final words in this scene chillingly mock the language of love and marriage: "I am your own forever" (III.iii.482).

ACT III, SCENE IV

SUMMARY

Desdemona orders the clown to find Cassio and bring him the message that she has made her suit to Othello. As the clown departs, Desdemona wonders to Emilia where her handkerchief might be. Othello enters and tells Desdemona to give him her hand. She does so, and he chastises her for her hand's moistness, which suggests sexual promiscuity. He then asks her to lend him her handkerchief. When Desdemona cannot produce the handkerchief he wants to see, Othello explains the handkerchief's history. An Egyptian sorceress gave it to his mother and told her that it would make her desirable and keep Othello's father loyal, but if she lost it or gave it away, Othello's father would leave her. Othello's mother gave him the magic handkerchief on her deathbed, instructing him to give it to the woman he desired to marry. Desdemona is unsettled by the story and says that she has the handkerchief, but not with her. Othello does not believe her. As he accuses her, demanding "The handkerchief!" with increasing vehemence, she entreats for Cassio as a way of changing the subject.

After Othello storms off, Emilia laments the fickleness of men. Cassio and Iago enter, and Cassio immediately continues with his suit to Desdemona for help. Desdemona tells Cassio that his timing is unfortunate, as Othello is in a bad humor, and Iago promises to go soothe his master. Emilia speculates that Othello is jealous, but Desdemona maintains her conviction that Othello is upset by some political matter. She tells Cassio to wait while she goes to find Othello and bring him to talk with his former lieutenant.

While Cassio waits, Bianca, a prostitute, enters. She reprimands him for not visiting her more frequently, and he apologizes, saying that he is under stress. He asks her to copy the embroidery of a handkerchief he recently found in his room onto another handkerchief. Bianca accuses him of making her copy the embroidery of a love gift from some other woman, but Cassio tells her she is being silly. They make a plan to meet later that evening.

ANALYSIS

In this scene, the time scheme of the play begins to unravel. When Bianca talks to Cassio, she says, "What, keep a week away," suggesting that Cassio has been on the island for at least a week (III. iv.168). But the play has only represented three days thus far: the first day in Venice, the day of the arrival and revels in Cyprus, and the day that begins at the beginning of Act III and continues until the end of the play. Critics and editors have named this problem the "double time scheme": two separate time frames operate simultaneously. This inconsistency is somewhat disorienting—like Othello, the audience feels stuck in a chaotic world. The events onstage are not only beyond our control, they defy logical understanding. For instance, it is difficult to understand how Desdemona could have had time to commit adultery.

From the moment it is introduced into the plot, the handkerchief given to Desdemona by Othello becomes the play's most important symbol. As a charmed gift given to Othello by his mother, the handkerchief represents Othello's mysterious and exotic heritage, a heritage that he has repudiated as a Christian and Venetian citizen. More immediately, to Othello the handkerchief represents Desdemona's chastity, and her giving it away is a sign that she has given her body away. In Act III, scene iii, Iago mentions that the handkerchief's much-discussed embroidery is a design of strawberries. The image of strawberries on a white background recalls the bloodstains on a wedding sheet that prove a bride's virginity; moreover, the dye used to color the strawberry pattern actually consists of the preserved blood of dead virgins. Thus, the handkerchief suggests a number of different interpretations. By positioning the handkerchief in Cassio's lodging, Iago as good as convicts Desdemona of unfaithfulness. And when, in the following scene, Bianca is found to be in possession of the handkerchief, instructed to copy the embroidery, Desdemona seems no better than a prostitute herself, carelessly allowing what was once a symbol of Othello's uniqueness to be passed around and replicated. Othello has convinced himself that Desdemona has lost her virtue because she has lost a symbol of that virtue.

Emilia, who betrays her privileged position as Desdemona's attendant by giving Iago the handkerchief, is an elusive character. Emilia seems to become loyal to her husband in a way she hasn't been in the past: she decides to give Iago the handkerchief after having denied his request "a hundred times," and she lies to Desdemona about not knowing the handkerchief's whereabouts. Yet later, in Act IV, scene ii, Emilia will attempt to convince Othello of Desdemona's loyalty. She seems deeply skeptical of and knowledgeable about men in general. She immediately recognizes that Othello is jealous, despite Desdemona's protests, and her comment that jealousy "is a monster / Begot upon itself, born on itself" (III.iv.156–157) echoes Iago's earlier remark that jealousy "is the green-eyed monster which doth mock / The meat it feeds on" (III.iii.170–171). Iago mentions at the beginning of the play that he suspects his wife of unfaithfulness, and on one level Iago and Emilia seem to work out their conflict vicariously through Othello and Desdemona. But Emilia also comments that men "are all but stomachs, and we are all but food. / They eat us hungrily, and when they are full, / They belch us" (III.iv.100–102). This comment supports a reading of Othello's jealousy as a way of justifying his rejection of Desdemona.

Act III, scene iv assumes the bizarre shape of a perverted trial. From the moment he enters, Othello plays the role of the prosecutor, demanding that Desdemona produce the handkerchief and accusing her of being a whore. Instead of defending herself against her husband's accusations, Desdemona responds by advocating Cassio's case, appealing to Othello as a judge of Cassio's character. The result is a shouting match, wherein husband and wife completely fail to communicate, Othello repeatedly screaming "The handkerchief!" while Desdemona enumerates Cassio's noble qualities, all of which Othello takes as testimony against her. He points to her moist hand as evidence of her inherently lascivious nature. Finally, the handkerchief itself is the strong circumstantial proof that Iago promised him.

By this point, the plot unfolds without any further assistance from Iago, although he is still involved in manipulating it in some way. He has thus far been so careful to inform the audience of his every plan that it seems like he must have anticipated every turn in the road. As with the characters onstage, Iago's power with the audience lies in his ability to make them believe he knows more than he does.

SUMMARY & ANALYSIS

ACT IV, SCENE I

SUMMARY

Othello and Iago enter in mid-conversation. Iago goads Othello by arguing that it is no crime for a woman to be naked with a man, if nothing happens. Iago then remarks that if he were to give his wife a handkerchief, it would be hers to do as she wished with it. These persistent insinuations of Desdemona's unfaithfulness work Othello into an incoherent frenzy. He focuses obsessively on the handkerchief and keeps pumping Iago for information about Cassio's comments to Iago. Finally, Iago says that Cassio has told him he has lain with Desdemona, and Othello "[f]alls down in a trance" (IV.i.41 stage direction).

Cassio enters, and Iago mentions that Othello has fallen into his second fit of epilepsy in two days. He warns Cassio to stay out of the way but tells him that he would like to speak once Othello has gone. Othello comes out of his trance, and Iago explains that Cassio stopped by and that he has arranged to speak with the ex-lieutenant. Iago orders Othello to hide nearby and observe Cassio's face during their conversation. Iago explains that he will make Cassio retell the story of where, when, how, and how often he has slept with Desdemona, and when he intends to do so again. When Othello withdraws, Iago informs the audience of his actual intention. He will joke with Cassio about the prostitute Bianca, so that Cassio will laugh as he tells the story of Bianca's pursuit of him. Othello will be driven mad, thinking that Cassio is joking with Iago about Desdemona.

The plan works: Cassio laughs uproariously as he tells Iago the details of Bianca's love for him, and even makes gestures in an attempt to depict her sexual advances. Just as Cassio says that he no longer wishes to see Bianca, she herself enters with the handkerchief and again accuses Cassio of giving her a love token given to him by another woman. Bianca tells Cassio that if he doesn't show up for supper with her that evening, he will never be welcome to come back again. Othello has recognized his handkerchief and, coming out of hiding when Cassio and Bianca are gone, wonders how he should murder his former lieutenant. Othello goes on to lament his hardheartedness and love for Desdemona, but Iago reminds him of his purpose. Othello has trouble reconciling his wife's delicacy, class, beauty, and allure with her adulterous actions. He suggests that he will poison his wife, but Iago advises him to strangle her in the bed that she contaminated through her infidelity. Iago also promises to arrange Cassio's death.

Desdemona enters with Lodovico, who has come from Venice with a message from the duke. Lodovico irritates Othello by inquiring about Cassio, and Desdemona irritates Othello by answering Lodovico's inquiries. The contents of the letter also upset Othello—he has been called back to Venice, with orders to leave Cassio as his replacement in Cyprus. When Desdemona hears the news that she will be leaving Cyprus, she expresses her happiness, whereupon Othello strikes her. Lodovico is horrified by Othello's loss of self-control, and asks Othello to call back Desdemona, who has left the stage. Othello does so, only to accuse her of being a false and promiscuous woman. He tells Lodovico that he will obey the duke's orders, commands Desdemona to leave, and storms off. Lodovico cannot believe that the Othello he has just seen is the same self-controlled man he once knew. He wonders whether Othello is mad, but Iago refuses to answer Lodovico's questions, telling him that he must see for himself.

ANALYSIS

With Othello striking his wife in public and storming out inarticulately, this scene is the reverse of Act II, scene iii, where, after calming the "Turk within" his brawling soldiers, Othello gently led his wife back to bed. Now, insofar as Turks represented savagery in early modern England, Othello has exposed his own inner Turk, and he brutally orders his wife to bed. Iago's lies have not only misled Othello, they have shifted him from his status of celebrated defender of Venice to cultural outsider and threat to Venetian security.

Lodovico's arrival from Venice serves as a reminder of how great Othello's transformation has been. As he stood before the senate at the beginning of the play, he was a great physical as well as verbal presence, towering above Brabanzio in stature and in eloquence, arresting the eyes and ears of his peers in the most political of public spaces, the court. After a short time in Cyprus, Iago has managed to bring about Othello's "savage madness" (IV.i.52). Othello loses control of his speech and, as he writhes on the ground, his movements. Othello's trance and swoon in this scene present him at the greatest possible distance from the noble figure he was before the senate in Act I, scene iii.

The action of the play takes place almost wholly in Iago's world, where appearances, rather than truth, are what count. Because of Iago's machinations, Cassio is perfectly placed to seem to give evidence of adultery, and Othello is perfectly placed to interpret whatever Cassio says or does as such. Throughout the play, Othello has been oblivious to speech, always sure that speech masks hidden meaning. Othello's obsession with appearances is the reason why he is content to *watch* Cassio's supposed confession, despite the fact that confessions are heard rather than seen. He also turns Lodovico's letters—which announce that Othello has been replaced by Cassio as governor of Cyprus in the same manner in which he believes Cassio has replaced him in the bedroom—into "ocular proof" that he is being supplanted.

Cyprus serves as a contrast to Venice, a place where the normal structures and laws governing civil society cease to operate. Such a world is common within Shakespeare's plays, though far more prevalent in his comedies. In *A Midsummer Night's Dream* and *As You Like It,* for example, the forest functions as an unstructured, malleable world in which the characters can transgress societal norms, work out their conflicts, and then return to society with no harm done. In the first act of *Othello,* Cyprus is clearly not such a world; it is a territory of Venice, to which Othello and company are called as a matter of state. As soon as the Turkish threat has been eliminated, however, the characters seem to lose their connection to Venetian society, and, with its festivities and drunken revelry, Cyprus then seems to have more in common with the alien, pastoral worlds of many of Shakespeare's comedies.

At many points, in fact, the plot of *Othello* resembles those of Shakespeare comedies in that it is based upon misrecognition and jealousy. The resemblances to comedy suggest that the misunderstandings of the play will be recognized and all will live happily ever after. But Cyprus, unlike the forest of *A Midsummer Night's Dream,* is still connected to Venetian society, and the arrival of Lodovico strengthens the Venetian presence and reminds Othello of the necessity of safeguarding his societal and political reputation. Cyprus, then, becomes a sort of trap, a false escape, in which the societal norms that seem to have disappeared reemerge to capture the transgressors. This mechanism of capture that exerts its force over the characters of Cyprus also occurs within Othello himself. The play refers on a number of occasions to jealousy as an innate force that cannot be planted, but instead grows from within and consumes itself and its host. Othello falls prey to the illusion of his own strength and power, and the jealousy it hides, just as Cyprus gives the illusion of providing a haven from the workings of the law.

Like Cyprus, Othello is half Venetian, half "other," and his predicament is the result of forces that are half comedic mischief and half deep-rooted, essential evil. Perhaps as a way of embodying these two clashing worlds, the play continues to upset the audience's relationship to time. Iago claims, "This is [Othello's] second fit. He had one yesterday" (IV.i.48). We have no basis on which to judge this claim, but if the play's action does, in fact, span three days, then Othello's first fit must have taken place before Iago even provoked his jealous rage. Similarly, when Bianca enters and chides Cassio for giving her a handkerchief she believes to be a love token from some other woman, she talks as though she never had almost the exact same conversation with Cassio in Act III, scene iv. The play's unrealistic lapses, repetitions, expansions, and contractions may contribute to the audience's sense that Iago's power is almost like that of a charmer invoking a kind of magic.

Act IV, scenes ii–iii

Summary: Act IV, scene ii

Othello interrogates Emilia about Desdemona's behavior, but Emilia insists that Desdemona has done nothing suspicious. Othello tells Emilia to summon Desdemona, implying while Emilia is gone that she is a "bawd," or female pimp (IV.ii.21). When Emilia returns with Desdemona, Othello sends Emilia to guard the door. Alone with Desdemona, Othello weeps and proclaims that he could have borne any affliction other than the pollution of the "fountain" from which his future children are to flow (IV.ii.61). When Desdemona fervently denies being unfaithful, Othello sarcastically replies that he begs her pardon: he took her for the "cunning whore of Venice" who married Othello (IV.ii.93). Othello storms out of the room, and Emilia comes in to comfort her mistress. Desdemona tells Emilia to lay her wedding sheets on the bed for that night.

At Desdemona's request, Emilia brings in Iago, and Desdemona tries to find out from him why Othello has been treating her like a whore. Emilia says to her husband that Othello must have been deceived by some villain, the same sort of villain who made Iago suspect Emilia of sleeping with Othello. Iago assures Desdemona that Othello is merely upset by some official business, and a trumpet flourish calls Emilia and Desdemona away to dinner with the Venetian emissaries.

Roderigo enters, furious that he is still frustrated in his love, and ready to make himself known in his suit to Desdemona so that she might return all of the jewels that Iago was supposed to have given her from him. Iago tells Roderigo that Cassio is being assigned to Othello's place. Iago also lies, saying that Othello is being sent to Mauritania, in Africa, although he is really being sent back to Venice. He tells Roderigo that the only way to prevent Othello from taking Desdemona away to Africa with him would be to get rid of Cassio. He sets about persuading Roderigo that he is just the man for "knocking out [Cassio's] brains" (IV.ii.229).

Summary: Act IV, scene iii

After dinner, Othello proposes to walk with Lodovico, and sends Desdemona to bed, telling her that he will be with her shortly and that she should dismiss Emilia. Desdemona seems aware of her imminent fate as she prepares for bed. She says that if she dies before Emilia, Emilia should use one of the wedding sheets for her shroud. As Emilia helps her mistress to undress, Desdemona sings a song, called "Willow," about a woman whose love forsook her. She says she learned the song from her mother's maid, Barbary, who died singing the song after she had been deserted by her lover. The song makes Desdemona think about adultery, and she asks Emilia whether she would cheat on her husband "for all the world" (IV.iii.62). Emilia says that she would not deceive her husband for jewels or rich clothes, but that the whole world is a huge prize and would outweigh the offense. This leads Emilia to speak about the fact that women have appetites for sex and infidelity just as men do, and that men who deceive their wives have only themselves to blame if their wives cheat on them. Desdemona replies that she prefers to answer bad deeds with good deeds rather than with more bad deeds. She readies herself for bed.

Analysis: Act IV, scenes ii–iii

In Act IV, scene ii, Othello interrogates Emilia as if she were a witness to a crime. Her testimony would be strong evidence of Desdemona's innocence, except that Othello dismisses it all as lies, because it does not accord with what he already believes. Just as there is no way for Othello to prove beyond any doubt that Desdemona has been unfaithful, no amount of evidence could now overturn Othello's belief in her guilt. (In the final scene, Othello does abruptly decide that he has been deceived all along by Iago, but not because he is confronted by compelling proof.) Othello explains away any evidence in Desdemona's favor, however strong, by imagining Emilia and Desdemona to be subtle and sophisticated liars.

When Othello has finished questioning Emilia, he interrogates Desdemona. She is still very much the articulate, generous wife she has been in earlier scenes, and she fervently denies Othello's accusations. Even though he has no intention of believing her, he calls on her to swear that she is honest, as if all he wants is to see her damn herself with more lies. Moreover, he exaggerates her infidelities out of all proportion to reality or human possibility, comparing her copulation to the breeding of summer flies or foul toads. Having opened the floodgates of doubt, Othello seems to have expanded Desdemona's infractions to make her the worst wife humanly conceivable. Perhaps any infidelity is as painful to him as a thousand infidelities, and his exaggerations only communicate the importance to him of her chastity. It is also possible that Othello's belief that Desdemona has been unfaithful has robbed him of his only stable point of reference, so that he has no grip on reality to check his imagination.

Having had to preside over a state dinner right after being abused by her husband in Act IV, scene ii, Desdemona must be completely exhausted by the beginning of Act IV, scene iii. She submits without complaint to Othello's order that she go to bed and dismiss Emilia. Despite Othello's repeated offenses, Desdemona continues to love her husband. Alone with Desdemona, Emilia reflects that it would have been better if Desdemona had never seen Othello, but Desdemona rejects this idea, saying that Othello seems noble and graceful to her, even in his rebukes.

As Emilia undresses her, Desdemona suddenly remarks that Lodovico, who was onstage at the beginning of the scene, "is a proper man" (IV.iii.34). This remark suggests that Lodovico is attractive, all that a man should be, and it is somewhat puzzling, considering all that Desdemona has to think about at this moment. She may simply be unable to think any further about the inexplicable disaster that has befallen her marriage. Or, she may be mulling over the implications of Emilia's idea: what would her life be like if she hadn't married Othello? Having just been violently rebuked for infidelity by her husband, Desdemona now seems to think for the first time about what it would mean to be unfaithful. As if reading

Desdemona's thought, Emilia runs with the suggestion of Lodovico's attractiveness, declaring that she knows a woman who would "walk barefoot to / Palestine for a touch of his nether lip" (IV.iii.36–37). Emilia's comment serves as an invitation for Desdemona to speak more openly about the possibility of her infidelity.

When Desdemona tells the story behind the "Willow" song that she sings, she says that the name of her mother's maid was "Barbary" (IV.iii.25), inadvertently echoing Iago's description of Othello as a "Barbary horse" (I.i.113). The word refers to the countries along the north coast of Africa, and thus the name suggests an exotic, African element in Desdemona's background, although the name "Barbary" was in use in Elizabethan England, so Barbary herself wasn't necessarily African. The song itself is melancholy, and it portrays an attitude of fatalism regarding love, a resigned acceptance of misfortune that Desdemona seems to embrace. "Let nobody blame him, his scorn I approve," she sings, before realizing that she has supplied the wrong words (IV.iii.50).

Desdemona's attitude toward her chastity represents what Renaissance males wanted and expected of women, and it is certainly what Othello wants from his wife. She sees it as an absolute entity that is worth more to her than her life or ownership of the entire whole world. Emilia, on the other hand, suggests that the ideal of female chastity is overblown and exaggerated. Throughout the scene, Emilia seems to be trying to gently hint that instead of quietly suffering Othello's abuse, Desdemona ought to look for happiness elsewhere. She argues that women are basically the same as men, and that the two sexes are unfaithful for the same reasons: affection for people other than their spouse, human weakness, and simple desire for enjoyment, or "sport" (IV.iii.95). Contrasted with Othello, who veers between seeing Desdemona as a monumentalized, ideal figure and as a whore with a thousand partners, Emilia's words do not advocate infidelity so much as a desire for reasonable middle ground, a societal acknowledgment that women are human beings with needs and desires rather than virgins or whores.

ACT V, SCENES I–II

SUMMARY: ACT V, SCENE I

Iago and Roderigo wait outside the brothel where Cassio visits Bianca. Iago positions Roderigo with a rapier (a type of sword) in a place where he will be able to ambush Cassio. Iago then withdraws himself, although Roderigo asks him not to go too far in case he needs help killing Cassio. Cassio enters, and Roderigo stabs at him but fails to pierce Cassio's armor. Cassio stabs and wounds Roderigo. Iago darts out in the commotion, stabs Cassio in the leg, and exits. Not knowing who has stabbed him, Cassio falls. At this moment, Othello enters. Hearing Cassio's cries of murder, Othello believes that Iago has killed him. Inspired by what he believes to be Iago's successful vengeance, Othello returns to his bedroom to kill Desdemona.

Lodovico and Graziano enter and hear Cassio's and Roderigo's cries. They can see nothing because of the darkness, and they are wary of helping the crying men in case it is a trap. Iago enters carrying a light. He first pretends to discover Cassio, who begs him for help, and then stumbles upon Cassio's assailant, Roderigo, whom Iago stabs without hesitation. Graziano and Lodovico are still unable to see Iago, and they are unaware of what he is doing. Finally, the three men come face-to-face, and they question Cassio about his injuries.

Bianca enters and begins to cry out when she sees the wounded Cassio. Iago questions Cassio about his assailant, but Cassio can provide no explanation for what has happened. Iago suggests that Roderigo is to blame. Cassio says that he does not know Roderigo. Attendants carry off Cassio and Roderigo's corpse. Emilia enters, and Iago tells her what has happened, adding the explanation, "This is the fruits of whoring" (V.i.118). He and Emilia chastise Bianca, at whose house Cassio had dined that evening. Iago takes Bianca under arrest, and sends Emilia to tell Othello and Desdemona what has happened. Iago ends the scene with an aside: "This is the night / That either makes me or fordoes [undoes] me quite" (V.i.130–131).

SUMMARY: ACT V, SCENE II

> Then must you speak
> Of one that loved not wisely but too well,
> Of one not easily jealous but, being wrought,
> Perplexed in the extreme; of one whose hand,
> Like the base Indian, threw a pearl away
> Richer than all his tribe....
>
> (See QUOTATIONS, p. 59)

Holding a candle, Othello stands over the sleeping Desdemona and prepares to kill her. He bends down to kiss her once before he does the deed, she wakes, and he tells her to prepare to die. Growing frightened, Desdemona asks her husband why he means to kill her, and Othello responds that she has been unfaithful to him with Cassio—he has seen the proof in the handkerchief. Othello refuses to believe Desdemona's denial of the charge, saying that Cassio has confessed but will speak no more, since he has been killed by Iago. Desdemona begins to weep for Cassio, which only drives Othello into a greater rage. Wrestling with her as she begs to be allowed to live just a little longer, Othello finally succeeds in smothering his wife. Emilia calls from outside the door, and Othello, apparently delirious, confuses her cries with his wife's and concludes that Desdemona is not yet dead. Thinking himself to be merciful, and not wanting to have his wife linger in pain, he smothers her again.

Othello draws the bed curtains and lets Emilia in. Emilia informs Othello that Cassio has killed Roderigo. Othello asks if Cassio has been killed as well, and Emilia informs him that Cassio is alive. As Othello begins to realize that his plans have gone awry, Desdemona cries out that she has been murdered. She stays alive long enough to recant this statement, telling Emilia that she was not murdered but killed herself. She dies. Othello triumphantly admits to Emilia that he killed Desdemona, and when she asks him why, Othello tells her that Iago opened his eyes to Desdemona's falsehood. Unfazed by Othello's threat that she "were best" to remain silent, Emilia calls out for help, bringing Montano, Graziano, and Iago to the scene (V.ii.168).

As the truth of Iago's villainy begins to come out through Emilia's accusations, Othello falls weeping upon the bed that contains the body of his dead wife. Almost to himself, Graziano expresses relief that Brabanzio is dead—the first news the audience has heard of this—and has not lived to see his daughter come to such a terrible end. Othello still clings to his belief in Iago's truth and Desdemona's guilt, mentioning the handkerchief and Cassio's "confession." When Othello mentions the handkerchief, Emilia erupts, and Iago, no longer certain that he can keep his plots hidden, attempts to silence her with his sword. Graziano stops him and Emilia explains how she found the handkerchief and gave it to Iago. Othello runs at Iago but is disarmed by Montano. In the commotion, Iago is able to stab his wife, who falls, apparently dying. Iago flees and is pursued by Montano and Graziano. Left alone onstage with the bodies of the two women, Othello searches for another sword. Emilia's dying words provide eerie background music, as she sings a snatch of the song "Willow." She tells Othello that Desdemona was chaste and loved him.

Graziano returns to find Othello armed and defiant, mourning the loss of his wife. They are joined shortly by Montano, Lodovico, Cassio, and Iago, who is being held prisoner. Othello stabs Iago, wounding him, and Lodovico orders some soldiers to disarm Othello. Iago sneers that he bleeds but is not killed. He refuses to say anything more about what he has done, but Lodovico produces a letter found in Roderigo's pocket that reveals everything that has happened. Seeking some kind of final reconciliation, Othello asks Cassio how he came by the handkerchief, and Cassio replies that he found it in his chamber.

Lodovico tells Othello that he must come with them back to Venice, and that he will be stripped of his power and command and put on trial. Refusing to be taken away before he has spoken, Othello asks his captors, "When you shall these unlucky deeds relate, / Speak of me as I am" (V.ii.350–351). He reminds them of a time in Aleppo when he served the Venetian state and slew a malignant Turk. "I took by the throat the circumcised dog / And smote him thus," says Othello, pulling a third dagger from hiding and stabbing himself in demonstration (V.ii.364–365). Pledging to "die upon a kiss," Othello falls onto the bed with his wife's body (V.ii.369).

Lodovico tells Iago to look at the result of his devious efforts, names Graziano as Othello's heir, and puts Montano in charge of Iago's execution. Lodovico prepares to leave for Venice to bear the news from Cyprus to the duke and senate.

ANALYSIS: ACT IV, SCENES I–II

In the first scene of Act V, we see the utterly futile end of Roderigo and his plans. Roderigo was first persuaded that he need only follow Othello and Desdemona to Cyprus in order to win over Desdemona, then that he need only disgrace Cassio, then that he need only *kill* Cassio. Now, Roderigo, stabbed by the man who gave him false hope, dies empty-handed in every possible way. He has given all his money and jewels to Iago, who admits that the jewelry more than anything else motivated his killing of Roderigo: "Live Roderigo, / He calls me to a restitution large / Of gold and jewels that I bobbed from him" (V.i.14–16). Roderigo is certainly a pathetic character, evidenced by the fact that he does not even succeed in killing Cassio. Unwittingly, Roderigo causes Iago's plan to be foiled for the first time in the play. Because of this, Iago is forced to bloody his own hands, also for the first time in the play. Displaying a talent for improvisation, Iago takes the burden of action into his own hands because he has no other choice. Once Iago sees that Roderigo has failed to kill Cassio, Iago is able to wound Cassio, return with a light to "save" Cassio, kill Roderigo, and cast suspicion on Bianca and her brothel, all in a very short time. Neither Lodovico, Graziano, nor Cassio shows the slightest suspicion that Iago is somehow involved in the mayhem. Othello is not the only one who finds Iago "honest."

Othello's brief appearance in Act V, scene i, is particularly horrifying. Joyfully supposing Cassio to be dead, Othello proceeds to his bedchamber with great fervor, crying, "Strumpet, I come. / Forth of my heart those charms, thine eyes, are blotted. / Thy bed, lust-stained, shall with lust's blood be spotted" (V.i.35–37). When he promises that the bed shall "with lust's blood be spotted," he means that when he kills Desdemona, her guilty blood of "lust" will spot the sheets. But spotted sheets also suggests wedding-night sex.

As Othello prepares to kill Desdemona at the beginning of the final scene, the idea of killing her becomes curiously intertwined, in his mind, with the idea of taking her virginity. In Act V, scene ii, he expresses his sorrow that he has to kill her in terms that suggest his reluctance to take her virginity: "When I have plucked thy rose / I cannot give it vital growth again. / It must needs wither" (V.ii.13–15). He steels himself to kill her, but he refuses to "shed her blood" or scar her white skin, which is as "smooth as monumental alabaster." His words imply that the real tragedy is the loss of her virginity, which would leave her irretrievably spoiled. Ironically, despite being convinced of her corruption, part of him seems to view her as still intact, like an alabaster statue or an unplucked rose. Furthermore, the reader may recall that the all-important handkerchief is dyed with the blood of *dead* virgins. The handkerchief's importance to Othello may suggest that he thinks it is better for a woman to die as a virgin than live as a wife.

Although it seems ludicrous to suggest that Othello has not yet taken Desdemona's virginity, the play includes two scenes during which their marriage is supposed to be sexually consummated, and in both the couple is interrupted as Othello is called on to resolve a crisis. This is only, it seems, the couple's third night together, and Desdemona has asked that her wedding sheets be put on the bed. The wedding sheets would prove one way or another whether the marriage was consummated, depending on whether they were stained with blood. Desdemona's choice of the sheets for a shroud may suggest that they are unstained. If they *have* consummated their marriage, Othello's words may suggest his unwillingness to accept the fact that he has already taken Desdemona's virginity, and his jealous fantasies about Desdemona's supposed debauchery may stem from his fear of her newly awakened sexuality, and from his own feeling of responsibility for having awakened it.

After Desdemona wakes, the scene progresses in a series of wavelike rushes that leave the audience as stunned and disoriented as the characters onstage. For starters, Desdemona seems to die twice—Othello smothers her once, then smothers her again after mistaking Emilia's screams from outside for his wife's. Astonishingly, Desdemona finds breath again to speak four final lines *after* Emilia enters the bedroom. Similarly, Emilia's death appears certain after Iago stabs her and Graziano says, "[T]he woman falls. Sure he hath killed his wife," and then, "He's gone, but his wife's killed" (V.ii.243, 245). Yet, eight lines later, Emilia speaks again, calling, "What did thy song bode, lady?" (V.ii.253). She speaks another five lines before dying for good.

Before he kills himself, Othello invokes his prior services to the state, asking Lodovico and the other Venetians to listen to him for a moment. At this point, he is resolved to die, and his concern is with how he will be remembered. When he appeals to his listeners to describe him as he actually is, neither better or worse, the audience may or may not agree with his characterization of himself as one not easily made jealous, or as one who loved "not wisely but too well" (V.ii.353). As he continues, though, he addresses an important problem: will his crime be remembered as the fall from grace of a Venetian Christian, or an assault on Venice by an ethnic and cultural outsider? He stresses his outsider status in a way that he does not do earlier in the play, comparing himself to a "base Indian" who cast away a pearl worth more than all of his tribe (V.ii.356–357). Finally, he recalls a time in which he defended Venice by smiting an enemy Turk, and then stabs himself in a reenactment of his earlier act, thereby casting himself as both insider and outsider, enemy of the state and defender of the state.

Throughout the play, Shakespeare cultivates Othello's ambivalent status as insider and outsider. Othello identifies himself firmly with Christian culture, yet his belief in fate and the charmed handkerchief suggest ties to a pagan heritage. Despite the fact that his Christianity seems slightly ambiguous, however, Shakespeare

repeatedly casts Othello as Christ and Iago as Judas (or, ironically, as Peter). (See analysis of Act I, scene ii, and Act III, scene iii.)
These echoes of the Gospel suggest that Othello and his tragedy are
somehow central to the Christian world of Venice. Moreover, while
most modern editions of the play include the words "base Indian"
(V.ii.356), the First Folio edition actually says "base Iudean" (i.e.,
Judean), possibly implying that Othello compares himself to Judas.
The play's rich biblical references suggest that Othello is both Christ
and Judas, a man who sacrifices himself to expiate the Venetians'
guilt as well as his own. What larger crime Othello's suicide atones
for, however, the audience can only conjecture.

IMPORTANT QUOTATIONS
EXPLAINED

1. Were I the Moor I would not be Iago.
    In following him I follow but myself;
    Heaven is my judge, not I for love and duty,
    But seeming so for my peculiar end.
    For when my outward action doth demonstrate
    The native act and figure of my heart
    In compliment extern, 'tis not long after
    But I will wear my heart upon my sleeve
    For daws to peck at. I am not what I am.

    (I.i.57–65)

In this early speech, Iago explains his tactics to Roderigo. He follows Othello not out of "love" or "duty," but because he feels he can exploit and dupe his master, thereby revenging himself upon the man he suspects of having slept with his wife. Iago finds that people who are what they seem are foolish. The day he decides to demonstrate outwardly what he feels inwardly, Iago explains, will be the day he makes himself most vulnerable: "I will wear my heart upon my sleeve / For daws to peck at." His implication, of course, is that such a day will never come.

This speech exemplifies Iago's cryptic and elliptical manner of speaking. Phrases such as "Were I the Moor I would not be Iago" and "I am not what I am" hide as much as, if not more than, they reveal. Iago is continually playing a game of deception, even with Roderigo and the audience. The paradox or riddle that the speech creates is emblematic of Iago's power throughout the play: his smallest sentences ("Think, my lord?" in III.iii.109) or gestures (beckoning Othello closer in Act IV, scene i) open up whole worlds of interpretation.

2.   My noble father,
      I do perceive here a divided duty.
      To you I am bound for life and education.
      My life and education both do learn me
      How to respect you. You are the lord of my duty,
      I am hitherto your daughter. But here's my husband,
      And so much duty as my mother showed
      To you, preferring you before her father,
      So much I challenge that I may profess
      Due to the Moor my lord.   (I.iii.179–188)

These words, which Desdemona speaks to her father before the Venetian senate, are her first of the play. Her speech shows her thoughtfulness, as she does not insist on her loyalty to Othello at the expense of respect for her father, but rather acknowledges that her duty is "divided." Because Desdemona is brave enough to stand up to her father and even partially rejects him in public, these words also establish for the audience her courage and her strength of conviction. Later, this same ability to separate different degrees and kinds of affection will make Desdemona seek, without hesitation, to help Cassio, thereby fueling Othello's jealousy. Again and again, Desdemona speaks clearly and truthfully, but, tragically, Othello is poisoned by Iago's constant manipulation of language and emotions and is therefore blind to Desdemona's honesty.

QUOTATIONS

3. Haply for I am black,
    And have not those soft parts of conversation
    That chamberers have; or for I am declined
    Into the vale of years—yet that's not much—
    She's gone. I am abused, and my relief
    Must be to loathe her. O curse of marriage,
    That we can call these delicate creatures ours
    And not their appetites! I had rather be a toad
    And live upon the vapor of a dungeon
    Than keep a corner in the thing I love
    For others' uses. Yet 'tis the plague of great ones;
    Prerogatived are they less than the base.
    'Tis destiny unshunnable, like death.   (III.iii.267–279)

When, in Act I, scene iii, Othello says that he is "rude" in speech, he shows that he does not really believe his own claim by going on to deliver a lengthy and very convincing speech about how he won Desdemona over with his wonderful storytelling (I.iii.81). However, after Iago has raised Othello's suspicions about his wife's fidelity, Othello seems to have at least partly begun to believe that he is inarticulate and barbaric, lacking "those soft parts of conversation / That chamberers [those who avoid practical labor and confine their activities to the 'chambers' of ladies] have." This is also the first time that Othello himself, and not Iago, calls negative attention to either his race or his age. His conclusion that Desdemona is "gone" shows how far Iago's insinuations about Cassio and Desdemona have taken Othello: in a matter of a mere 100 lines or so, he has progressed from belief in his conjugal happiness to belief in his abandonment.

The ugly imagery that follows this declaration of abandonment—Othello finds Desdemona to be a mere "creature" of "appetite" and imagines himself as a "toad" in a "dungeon"—anticipates his later speech in Act IV, scene ii, in which he compares Desdemona to a "cistern for foul toads / To knot and gender in," and says that she is as honest "as summer flies are in the shambles [slaughterhouses], / That quicken even with blowing" (IV.ii.63–64, 68–69). Othello's comment, "'tis the plague of great ones," shows that the only potential comfort Othello finds in his moment of hopelessness is his success as a soldier, which proves that he is not "base." He attempts to consider his wife's purported infidelity as an inevitable part of his being a great man, but his comfort is halfhearted and unconvincing, and he concludes by resigning himself to cuckoldry as though it were "death."

4. I am glad I have found this napkin.
    This was her first remembrance from the Moor,
    My wayward husband hath a hundred times
    Wooed me to steal it, but she so loves the token—
    For he conjured her she should ever keep it—
    That she reserves it evermore about her
    To kiss and talk to. I'll ha' the work ta'en out,
    And give't Iago. What he will do with it,
    Heaven knows, not I.
    I nothing, but to please his fantasy.   (III.iii.294–303)

This speech of Emilia's announces the beginning of *Othello*'s "handkerchief plot," a seemingly insignificant event—the dropping of a
handkerchief—that becomes the means by which Othello, Desdemona, Cassio, Roderigo, Emilia, and even Iago himself are completely undone. Before Othello lets the handkerchief fall from his
brow, we have neither heard of nor seen it. The primary function of
Emilia's speech is to explain the prop's importance: as the first gift
Othello gave Desdemona, it represents their oldest and purest feelings for one another.

While the fact that Iago "hath a hundred times / Wooed me to
steal it" immediately tips off the audience to the handkerchief's im-
minently prominent place in the tragic sequence of events, Emilia
seems entirely unsuspicious. To her, the handkerchief is literally a
trifle, "light as air," and this is perhaps why she remains silent about
the handkerchief's whereabouts even when Desdemona begins to
suffer for its absence. It is as though Emilia cannot, or refuses to,
imagine that her husband would want the handkerchief for any devious reason. Many critics have found Emilia's silence about the
handkerchief—and in fact the entire handkerchief plot—a great im-
plausibility, and it is hard to disagree with this up to a point. At the
same time, however, it serves as yet another instance in which Iago
has the extraordinary power to make those around him see only
what they want to see, and thereby not suspect what is obviously
suspicious.

5.   Then must you speak
     Of one that loved not wisely but too well,
     Of one not easily jealous but, being wrought,
     Perplexed in the extreme; of one whose hand,
     Like the base Indian, threw a pearl away
     Richer than all his tribe; of one whose subdued eyes,
     Albeit unused to the melting mood,
     Drop tears as fast as the Arabian trees
     Their medicinable gum. Set you down this,
     And say besides that in Aleppo once,
     Where a malignant and a turbaned Turk
     Beat a Venetian and traduced the state,
     I took by th' throat the circumcised dog
     And smote him thus.   (V.ii.352–365)

With these final words, Othello stabs himself in the chest. In this farewell speech, Othello reaffirms his position as a figure who is simultaneously a part of and excluded from Venetian society. The smooth eloquence of the speech and its references to "Arabian trees," "Aleppo," and a "malignant and a turbaned Turk" remind us of Othello's long speech in Act I, scene iii, lines 127–168, and of the tales of adventure and war with which he wooed Desdemona. No longer inarticulate with grief as he was when he cried, "O fool! fool! fool!," Othello seems to have calmed himself and regained his dignity and, consequently, our respect (V.ii.332). He reminds us once again of his martial prowess, the quality that made him famous in Venice. At the same time, however, by killing himself as he is describing the killing of a Turk, Othello identifies himself with those who pose a military—and, according to some, a psychological—threat to Venice, acknowledging in the most powerful and awful way the fact that he is and will remain very much an outsider. His suicide is a kind of martyrdom, a last act of service to the state, as he kills the only foe he has left to conquer: himself.

KEY FACTS

FULL TITLE

The Tragedy of Othello, the Moor of Venice

AUTHOR

William Shakespeare

TYPE OF WORK

Play

GENRE

Tragedy

LANGUAGE

English

TIME AND PLACE WRITTEN

Between 1601 and 1604, England

DATE OF FIRST PUBLICATION

1622

PUBLISHER

Thomas Walkley

TONE

Shakespeare clearly views the events of the play as tragic. He seems to view the marriage between Desdemona and Othello as noble and heroic, for the most part.

SETTING (TIME)

Late sixteenth century, during the wars between Venice and Turkey

SETTING (PLACE)

Venice in Act I; the island of Cyprus thereafter

PROTAGONIST

Othello

MAJOR CONFLICT

Othello and Desdemona marry and attempt to build a life together, despite their differences in age, race, and experience.

Their marriage is sabotaged by the envious Iago, who convinces Othello that Desdemona is unfaithful.

RISING ACTION

Iago tells the audience of his scheme, arranges for Cassio to lose his position as lieutenant, and gradually insinuates to Othello that Desdemona is unfaithful.

CLIMAX

The climax occurs at the end of Act III, scene iii, when Othello kneels with Iago and vows not to change course until he has achieved bloody revenge.

FALLING ACTION

Iago plants the handkerchief in Cassio's room and later arranges a conversation with Cassio, which Othello watches and sees as "proof" that Cassio and Desdemona have slept together. Iago unsuccessfully attempts to kill Cassio, and Othello smothers Desdemona with a pillow. Emilia exposes Iago's deceptions, Othello kills himself, and Iago is taken away to be tortured.

THEMES

The incompatibility of military heroism and love; the danger of isolation

MOTIFS

Sight and blindness; plants; animals; hell, demons, and monsters

SYMBOLS

The handkerchief; the song "Willow"

FORESHADOWING

Othello and Desdemona's speeches about love foreshadow the disaster to come; Othello's description of his past and of his wooing of Desdemona foreshadow his suicide speech; Desdemona's "Willow" song and remarks to Emilia in Act IV, scene iii, foreshadow her death.

KEY FACTS

STUDY QUESTIONS

1. *To what extent does Othello's final speech affect our assessment of him? What is the effect of his final anecdote about the Turk?*

Certainly, Othello's final speech is not all that one might wish for—his claim to be "one not easily jealous" is open to question, and his claim that he "loved not wisely but too well" seems both an understatement and an exaggeration (V.ii.354, 353). Further, Othello's invocation of his own military triumphs might be seen as another example of Othello dangerously misordering his priorities. He seems to position his political reputation as his biggest concern, as he did in Act III, scene iii, lines 353–355, when, having decided that Desdemona does not love him, he exclaimed, "Farewell the tranquil mind, farewell content, / Farewell the plumed troop and the big wars / That make ambition virtue."

At the same time, however, Othello's final speech does seem to restore to him somewhat the nobility that characterized him at the beginning of the play. From almost the first time he opens his mouth, Othello demonstrates—and the other characters confirm—his hypnotic eloquence when he speaks about his exploits in battle. Othello's final speech puts us in mind of his long speech in Act I, scene iii, so that we see him, even if only for a moment, as we saw him then. This process of conflating two different times and views of Othello is similar to the rhetorical effect achieved by Othello's dying words, where he makes his suicide seem a noble and heroic deed by conflating it with the killing of a Turk in service of the state.

2. *What role does incoherent language play in* OTHELLO? *How does Othello's language change over the course of the play? Pay particular attention to the handkerchief scene in Act III, scene iii, and Othello's fit in Act IV, scene i.*

At the beginning of the play, Othello has such confidence in his skill with language that he can claim that he is "rude" in speech, knowing that no one will possibly believe him (I.iii.81). He then dazzles his audience with a forty-line speech that effortlessly weaves words such as "hair-breadth" and "Anthropophagi" into blank verse lines. But in the moments when the pressure applied by Iago is particularly extreme, Othello's language deteriorates into fragmented, hesitant, and incoherent syntax. Throughout Act III, scene iii, Othello speaks in short, clipped exclamations and half-sentences such as "Ha!" (III.iii.169), "O misery!" (III.iii.175), and "Dost thou say so?" (III.iii.209). There is also notable repetition, as in "Not a jot, not a jot" (III.iii.219), "O, monstrous, monstrous!" (III.iii.431), "O, blood, blood, blood!" (III.iii.455), and "Damn her, lewd minx! O, damn her, damn her!" (III.iii.478).

Such moments, when Othello shifts from his typical seemingly effortless verse to near inarticulateness, demonstrate the extent to which Othello's passion has broken down his self-control. In Act III, scene iii, he is still speaking in mostly coherent sentences or phrases; but this is no longer the case in Act IV, scene i. This scene begins with Iago saying, "Will you think so?" and Othello can only helplessly and automatically echo, "Think so, Iago?" (IV.i.1–2). Iago then introduces the word "lie" into the conversation, which sends Othello into a frenzy as he attempts to sort out the semantic differences between Cassio "lying on" (that is, lying about) Desdemona and "lying with" (that is, having sex with) her (IV.i.33–35). The various words and images Iago has planted in Othello's mind over the course of the play are transformed into impressionistic, sporadic eruptions out of Othello's mouth: "Lie with her? 'Swounds, that's fulsome! Handkerchief—confessions—handkerchief" (IV.i.35–36). These eruptions culminate in the nonsense of "Pish! Noses, ears, and lips!" (IV.i.40). Ultimately, Othello's inability to articulate seems to overcome him physically, as he collapses "in a trance" (IV.i.41, stage direction).

3. *Analyze Desdemona's role. To what extent is she merely
a passive victim of Othello's brutality? How does her
character change when she is not with Othello?*

At the end of *Othello,* Desdemona seems to be the most passive kind
of victim. Smothered, deprived of breath and of words by her husband, she is totally overwhelmed by Othello's insane jealousy and
physical strength. But before her murder, Desdemona is remarkable
for showing more passivity when her husband is *not* around and
more assertiveness when he is.

Desdemona's first speech, in which she defends her recent marriage, is confident and forthright. When she gives it, she is the only
female character onstage, surrounded by powerful men who include
the duke, her husband, and her father, but she is not ashamed to as-
sert her belief in the validity of her desires and actions. Unfortunately,
Iago recognizes Desdemona's forthrightness and uses it against her.
He exploits her willingness to demand and justify what she wants
by making Cassio her cause and, simultaneously, Othello's enemy.
In Act III, scene iii, Desdemona asks Othello to forgive Cassio and
persists, in spite of Othello's rising consternation, until her husband
declares, "I will deny thee nothing" (III.iii. 41–84). Her courage is
apparent in her refusal to search for the missing handkerchief in Act
III, scene iv; in her willingness to shout back at Othello as he abuses
her in Act IV, scene i; and in her insistence upon her innocence in
Act V, scene ii. Her audacity seems to infuriate Othello all the more,
as what he takes to be shameless lies convince him that she is unre-
morseful in what he believes to be her sin.

The terrible effect of Othello's brutality is most obvious in Desdemona's scenes with Emilia. Emilia is cynical and bawdy, and she
gives Desdemona every possible opportunity to bad-mouth Othello.
Men, she says in Act III, scene iv, "are all but stomachs, and we all
but food. / They eat us hungrily, and when they are full, / They
belch us" (III.iv.100–102). Later, she insults Othello: "He called her
whore. A beggar in his drink / Could not have laid such terms upon
his callet [whore]" (IV.ii.124–125). And, at the end of Act IV, scene
iii, she gives a lengthy discourse about the virtues of infidelity. Desdemona, however, never says anything worse than "Heaven keep
the monster [jealousy] from Othello's mind" (III.iv.158). With her
closest confidante, Desdemona does not speak ill of her husband,
even as she shows the strain of his terrible abuse.

How to Write
Literary Analysis

The Literary Essay: A Step-by-Step Guide

When you read for pleasure, your only goal is enjoyment. You might find yourself reading to get caught up in an exciting story, to learn about an interesting time or place, or just to pass time. Maybe you're looking for inspiration, guidance, or a reflection of your own life. There are as many different, valid ways of reading a book as there are books in the world.

When you read a work of literature in an English class, however, you're being asked to read in a special way: you're being asked to perform *literary analysis*. To analyze something means to break it down into smaller parts and then examine how those parts work, both individually and together. Literary analysis involves examining all the parts of a novel, play, short story, or poem—elements such as character, setting, tone, and imagery—and thinking about how the author uses those elements to create certain effects.

A literary essay isn't a book review: you're not being asked whether or not you liked a book or whether you'd recommend it to another reader. A literary essay also isn't like the kind of book report you wrote when you were younger, where your teacher wanted you to summarize the book's action. A high school- or college-level literary essay asks, "How does this piece of literature actually work?" "How does it do what it does?" and, "Why might the author have made the choices he or she did?"

The Seven Steps
No one is born knowing how to analyze literature; it's a skill you learn and a process you can master. As you gain more practice with this kind of thinking and writing, you'll be able to craft a method that works best for you. But until then, here are seven basic steps to writing a well-constructed literary essay:

  1. Ask questions
  2. Collect evidence
  3. Construct a thesis

65

4. Develop and organize arguments
5. Write the introduction
6. Write the body paragraphs
7. Write the conclusion

---

1. ASK QUESTIONS

When you're assigned a literary essay in class, your teacher will often provide you with a list of writing prompts. Lucky you! Now all you have to do is choose one. Do yourself a favor and pick a topic that interests you. You'll have a much better (not to mention easier) time if you start off with something you enjoy thinking about. If you are asked to come up with a topic by yourself, though, you might start to feel a little panicked. Maybe you have too many ideas—or none at all. Don't worry. Take a deep breath and start by asking yourself these questions:

- **What struck you?** Did a particular image, line, or scene linger in your mind for a long time? If it fascinated you, chances are you can draw on it to write a fascinating essay.

- **What confused you?** Maybe you were surprised to see a character act in a certain way, or maybe you didn't understand why the book ended the way it did. Confusing moments in a work of literature are like a loose thread in a sweater: if you pull on it, you can unravel the entire thing. Ask yourself why the author chose to write about that character or scene the way he or she did and you might tap into some important insights about the work as a whole.

- **Did you notice any patterns?** Is there a phrase that the main character uses constantly or an image that repeats throughout the book? If you can figure out how that pattern weaves through the work and what the significance of that pattern is, you've almost got your entire essay mapped out.

- **Did you notice any contradictions or ironies?** Great works of literature are complex; great literary essays recognize and explain those complexities. Maybe the title (*Happy Days*) totally disagrees with the book's subject matter (hungry orphans dying in the woods). Maybe the main character acts one way around his family and a completely different way around his friends and associates. If you can find a way to explain a work's contradictory elements, you've got the seeds of a great essay.

At this point, you don't need to know exactly what you're going to say about your topic; you just need a place to begin your exploration. You can help direct your reading and brainstorming by formulating your topic as a *question,* which you'll then try to answer in your essay. The best questions invite critical debates and discussions, not just a rehashing of the summary. Remember, you're looking for something you can *prove or argue* based on evidence you find in the text. Finally, remember to keep the scope of your question in mind: is this a topic you can adequately address within the word or page limit you've been given? Conversely, is this a topic big enough to fill the required length?

GOOD QUESTIONS
> *"Are Romeo and Juliet's parents responsible for the deaths of their children?"*
> *"Why do pigs keep showing up in* LORD OF THE FLIES*?"*
> *"Are Dr. Frankenstein and his monster alike? How?"*

BAD QUESTIONS
> *"What happens to Scout in* TO KILL A MOCKINGBIRD*?"*
> *"What do the other characters in* JULIUS CAESAR *think about Caesar?"*
> *"How does Hester Prynne in* THE SCARLET LETTER *remind me of my sister?"*

---

2. COLLECT EVIDENCE

Once you know what question you want to answer, it's time to scour the book for things that will help you answer the question. Don't worry if you don't know what you want to say yet—right now you're just collecting ideas and material and letting it all percolate. Keep track of passages, symbols, images, or scenes that deal with your topic. Eventually, you'll start making connections between these examples and your thesis will emerge.

Here's a brief summary of the various parts that compose each and every work of literature. These are the elements that you will analyze in your essay, and which you will offer as evidence to support your arguments. For more on the parts of literary works, see the Glossary of Literary Terms at the end of this section.

LITERARY ANALYSIS

ELEMENTS OF STORY   These are the *what*s of the work—what happens, where it happens, and to whom it happens.

- **Plot:** All of the events and actions of the work.

- **Character:** The people who act and are acted upon in a literary work. The main character of a work is known as the *protagonist.*

- **Conflict:** The central tension in the work. In most cases, the protagonist wants something, while opposing forces (antagonists) hinder the protagonist's progress.

- **Setting:** When and where the work takes place. Elements of setting include location, time period, time of day, weather, social atmosphere, and economic conditions.

- **Narrator:** The person telling the story. The narrator may straightforwardly report what happens, convey the subjective opinions and perceptions of one or more characters, or provide commentary and opinion in his or her own voice.

- **Themes:** The main idea or message of the work—usually an abstract idea about people, society, or life in general. A work may have many themes, which may be in tension with one another.

ELEMENTS OF STYLE   These are the *how*s—how the characters speak, how the story is constructed, and how language is used throughout the work.

- **Structure and organization:** How the parts of the work are assembled. Some novels are narrated in a linear, chronological fashion, while others skip around in time. Some plays follow a traditional three- or five-act structure, while others are a series of loosely connected scenes. Some authors deliberately leave gaps in their works, leaving readers to puzzle out the missing information. A work's structure and organization can tell you a lot about the kind of message it wants to convey.

- **Point of view:** The perspective from which a story is told. In *first-person point of view,* the narrator involves him or herself in the story. ("I went to the store"; "We watched in horror as the bird slammed into the window.") A first-person narrator is usually the protagonist of the work, but not always. In *third-person point of view,* the narrator does not participate in the story. A third-person narrator may closely follow a specific character, recounting that individual character's thoughts or experiences, or it may be what we call an *omniscient* narrator. Omniscient narrators see and know all: they can witness any event in any time or place and are privy to the inner thoughts and feelings of all characters. Remember that the narrator and the author are not the same thing!

- **Diction:** Word choice. Whether a character uses dry, clinical language or flowery prose with lots of exclamation points can tell you a lot about his or her attitude and personality.

- **Syntax:** Word order and sentence construction. Syntax is a crucial part of establishing an author's narrative voice. Ernest Hemingway, for example, is known for writing in very short, straightforward sentences, while James Joyce characteristically wrote in long, incredibly complicated lines.

- **Tone:** The mood or feeling of the text. Diction and syntax often contribute to the tone of a work. A novel written in short, clipped sentences that use small, simple words might feel brusque, cold, or matter-of-fact.

- **Imagery:** Language that appeals to the senses, representing things that can be seen, smelled, heard, tasted, or touched.

- **Figurative language:** Language that is not meant to be interpreted literally. The most common types of figurative language are *metaphors* and *similes,* which compare two unlike things in order to suggest a similarity between them— for example, "All the world's a stage," or "The moon is like a ball of green cheese." (Metaphors say one thing *is* another thing; similes claim that one thing is *like* another thing.)

---

3. Construct a Thesis

When you've examined all the evidence you've collected and know how you want to answer the question, it's time to write your thesis statement. A *thesis* is a claim about a work of literature that needs to be supported by evidence and arguments. The thesis statement is the heart of the literary essay, and the bulk of your paper will be spent trying to prove this claim. A good thesis will be:

- **Arguable.** "*The Great Gatsby* describes New York society in the 1920s" isn't a thesis—it's a fact.

LITERARY ANALYSIS

- **Provable through textual evidence.** "*Hamlet* is a confusing but ultimately very well-written play" is a weak thesis because it offers the writer's personal opinion about the book. Yes, it's arguable, but it's not a claim that can be proved or supported with examples taken from the play itself.

- **Surprising.** "Both George and Lenny change a great deal in *Of Mice and Men*" is a weak thesis because it's obvious. A really strong thesis will argue for a reading of the text that is not immediately apparent.

- **Specific.** "Dr. Frankenstein's monster tells us a lot about the human condition" is *almost* a really great thesis statement, but it's still too vague. What does the writer mean by "a lot"? *How* does the monster tell us so much about the human condition?

GOOD THESIS STATEMENTS

Question: In *Romeo and Juliet*, which is more powerful in shaping the lovers' story: fate or foolishness?

Thesis: "Though Shakespeare defines Romeo and Juliet as 'star-crossed lovers' and images of stars and planets appear throughout the play, a closer examination of that celestial imagery reveals that the stars are merely witnesses to the characters' foolish activities and not the causes themselves."

Question: How does the bell jar function as a symbol in Sylvia Plath's *The Bell Jar*?

Thesis: "A bell jar is a bell-shaped glass that has three basic uses: to hold a specimen for observation, to contain gases, and to maintain a vacuum. The bell jar appears in each of these capacities in *The Bell Jar*, Plath's semi-autobiographical novel, and each appearance marks a different stage in Esther's mental breakdown."

Question: Would Piggy in *The Lord of the Flies* make a good island leader if he were given the chance?

Thesis: "Though the intelligent, rational, and innovative Piggy has the mental characteristics of a good leader, he ultimately lacks the social skills necessary to be an effective one. Golding emphasizes this point by giving Piggy a foil in the charismatic Jack, whose magnetic personality allows him to capture and wield power effectively, if not always wisely."

4. DEVELOP AND ORGANIZE ARGUMENTS

The reasons and examples that support your thesis will form the middle paragraphs of your essay. Since you can't really write your thesis statement until you know how you'll structure your argument, you'll probably end up working on steps 3 and 4 at the same time.

There's no single method of argumentation that will work in every context. One essay prompt might ask you to compare and contrast two characters, while another asks you to trace an image through a given work of literature. These questions require different kinds of answers and therefore different kinds of arguments. Below, we'll discuss three common kinds of essay prompts and some strategies for constructing a solid, well-argued case.

TYPES OF LITERARY ESSAYS

- **Compare and contrast**

    Compare and contrast the characters of Huck and Jim in THE ADVENTURES OF HUCKLEBERRY FINN.

    Chances are you've written this kind of essay before. In an academic literary context, you'll organize your arguments the same way you would in any other class. You can either go *subject by subject* or *point by point*. In the former, you'll discuss one character first and then the second. In the latter, you'll choose several traits (attitude toward life, social status, images and metaphors associated with the character) and devote a paragraph to each. You may want to use a mix of these two approaches—for example, you may want to spend a paragraph a piece broadly sketching Huck's and Jim's personalities before transitioning into a paragraph or two that describes a few key points of comparison. This can be a highly effective strategy if you want to make a counterintuitive argument—that, despite seeming to be totally different, the two objects being compared are actually similar in a very important way (or vice versa). Remember that your essay should reveal something fresh or unexpected about the text, so think beyond the obvious parallels and differences.

- **Trace**

    Choose an image—for example, birds, knives, or eyes—and trace that image throughout MACBETH.

    Sounds pretty easy, right? All you need to do is read the play, underline every appearance of a knife in *Macbeth,* and then list them in your essay in the order they appear, right? Well, not exactly. Your teacher doesn't want a simple catalog of examples. He or she wants to see you make *connections* between those examples—that's the difference between summarizing and analyzing. In the *Macbeth* example above, think about the different contexts in which knives appear in the play and to what effect. In *Macbeth,* there are real knives and imagined knives; knives that kill and knives that simply threaten. Categorize and classify your examples to give them some order. Finally, always keep the overall effect in mind. After you choose and analyze your examples, you should come to some greater understanding about the work, as well as your chosen image, symbol, or phrase's role in developing the major themes and stylistic strategies of that work.

- **Debate**

  Is the society depicted in 1984 good for its citizens?

  In this kind of essay, you're being asked to debate a moral, ethical, or aesthetic issue regarding the work. You might be asked to judge a character or group of characters (*Is Caesar responsible for his own demise?*) or the work itself (*Is* JANE EYRE *a feminist novel?*). For this kind of essay, there are two important points to keep in mind. First, don't simply base your arguments on your personal feelings and reactions. Every literary essay expects you to read and analyze the work, so search for evidence in the text. What do characters in *1984* have to say about the government of Oceania? What images does Orwell use that might give you a hint about his attitude toward the government? As in any debate, you also need to make sure that you define all the necessary terms before you begin to argue your case. What does it mean to be a "good" society? What makes a novel "feminist"? You should define your terms right up front, in the first paragraph after your introduction.

  Second, remember that strong literary essays make contrary and surprising arguments. Try to think outside the box. In the *1984* example above, it seems like the obvious answer would be no, the totalitarian society depicted in Orwell's novel is *not* good for its citizens. But can you think of any arguments for the opposite side? Even if your final assertion is that the novel depicts a cruel, repressive, and therefore harmful society, acknowledging and responding to the counterargument will strengthen your overall case.

5. WRITE THE INTRODUCTION

Your introduction sets up the entire essay. It's where you present your topic and articulate the particular issues and questions you'll be addressing. It's also where you, as the writer, introduce yourself to your readers. A persuasive literary essay immediately establishes its writer as a knowledgeable, authoritative figure.

An introduction can vary in length depending on the over-all length of the essay, but in a traditional five-paragraph essay it should be no longer than one paragraph. However long it is, your introduction needs to:

- **Provide any necessary context.** Your introduction should situate the reader and let him or her know what to expect. What book are you discussing? Which characters? What topic will you be addressing?

- **Answer the "So what?" question.** Why is this topic important, and why is your particular position on the topic noteworthy? Ideally, your introduction should pique the reader's interest by suggesting how your argument is surprising or otherwise counterintuitive. Literary essays make unexpected connections and reveal less-than-obvious truths.

- **Present your thesis.** This usually happens at or very near the end of your introduction.

- **Indicate the shape of the essay to come.** Your reader should finish reading your introduction with a good sense of the scope of your essay as well as the path you'll take toward proving your thesis. You don't need to spell out every step, but you do need to suggest the organizational pattern you'll be using.

Your introduction should not:

- **Be vague.** Beware of the two killer words in literary analysis: *interesting* and *important*. Of course the work, question, or example is interesting and important—that's why you're writing about it!

- **Open with any grandiose assertions.** Many student readers think that beginning their essays with a flamboyant statement such as, "Since the dawn of time, writers have been fascinated with the topic of free will," makes them sound important and commanding. You know what? It actually sounds pretty amateurish.

- **Wildly praise the work.** Another typical mistake student writers make is extolling the work or author. Your teacher doesn't need to be told that "Shakespeare is perhaps the greatest writer in the English language." You can mention a work's reputation in passing—by referring to *The Adventures of Huckleberry Finn* as "Mark Twain's enduring classic," for example—but don't make a point of bringing it up unless that reputation is key to your argument.

- **Go off-topic.** Keep your introduction streamlined and to the point. Don't feel the need to throw in all kinds of bells and whistles in order to impress your reader—just get to the point as quickly as you can, without skimping on any of the required steps.

6. Write the Body Paragraphs

Once you've written your introduction, you'll take the arguments you developed in step 4 and turn them into your body paragraphs. The organization of this middle section of your essay will largely be determined by the argumentative strategy you use, but no matter how you arrange your thoughts, your body paragraphs need to do the following:

- **Begin with a strong topic sentence.** Topic sentences are like signs on a highway: they tell the reader where they are and where they're going. A good topic sentence not only alerts readers to what issue will be discussed in the following paragraph but also gives them a sense of what argument will be made *about* that issue. "Rumor and gossip play an important role in *The Crucible*" isn't a strong topic sentence because it doesn't tell us very much. "The community's constant gossiping creates an environment that allows false accusations to flourish" is a much stronger topic sentence— it not only tells us *what* the paragraph will discuss (gossip) but *how* the paragraph will discuss the topic (by showing how gossip creates a set of conditions that leads to the play's climactic action).

- **Fully and completely develop a single thought.** Don't skip around in your paragraph or try to stuff in too much material. Body paragraphs are like bricks: each individual one needs to be strong and sturdy or the entire structure will collapse. Make sure you have really proven your point before moving on to the next one.

- **Use transitions effectively.** Good literary essay writers know that each paragraph must be clearly and strongly linked to the material around it. Think of each paragraph as a response to the one that precedes it. Use transition words and phrases such as *however, similarly, on the contrary, therefore*, and *furthermore* to indicate what kind of response you're making.

---

7. WRITE THE CONCLUSION

Just as you used the introduction to ground your readers in the topic before providing your thesis, you'll use the conclusion to quickly summarize the specifics learned thus far and then hint at the broader implications of your topic. A good conclusion will:

- **Do more than simply restate the thesis.** If your thesis argued that *The Catcher in the Rye* can be read as a Christian allegory, don't simply end your essay by saying, "And that is why *The Catcher in the Rye* can be read as a Christian allegory." If you've constructed your arguments well, this kind of statement will just be redundant.

- **Synthesize the arguments, not summarize them.** Similarly, don't repeat the details of your body paragraphs in your conclusion. The reader has already read your essay, and chances are it's not so long that they've forgotten all your points by now.

- **Revisit the "So what?" question.** In your introduction, you made a case for why your topic and position are important. You should close your essay with the same sort of gesture. What do your readers know now that they didn't know before? How will that knowledge help them better appreciate or understand the work overall?

- **Move from the specific to the general.** Your essay has most likely treated a very specific element of the work—a single character, a small set of images, or a particular passage. In your conclusion, try to show how this narrow discussion has wider implications for the work overall. If your essay on *To Kill a Mockingbird* focused on the character of Boo Radley, for example, you might want to include a bit in your conclusion about how he fits into the novel's larger message about childhood, innocence, or family life.

- **Stay relevant.** Your conclusion should suggest new directions of thought, but it shouldn't be treated as an opportunity to pad your essay with all the extra, interesting ideas you came up with during your brainstorming sessions but couldn't fit into the essay proper. Don't attempt to stuff in unrelated queries or too many abstract thoughts.

- **Avoid making overblown closing statements.** A conclusion should open up your highly specific, focused discussion, but it should do so without drawing a sweeping lesson about life or human nature. Making such observations may be part of the point of reading, but it's almost always a mistake in essays, where these observations tend to sound overly dramatic or simply silly.

A+ Essay Checklist

Congratulations! If you've followed all the steps we've outlined above, you should have a solid literary essay to show for all your efforts. What if you've got your sights set on an A+? To write the kind of superlative essay that will be rewarded with a perfect grade, keep the following rubric in mind. These are the qualities that teachers expect to see in a truly A+ essay. How does yours stack up?

- ✓ Demonstrates a thorough understanding of the book
- ✓ Presents an original, compelling argument
- ✓ Thoughtfully analyzes the text's formal elements
- ✓ Uses appropriate and insightful examples
- ✓ Structures ideas in a logical and progressive order
- ✓ Demonstrates a mastery of sentence construction, transitions, grammar, spelling, and word choice

Suggested Essay Topics

1. *Discuss the importance of setting in the play, paying close attention to physical details that differentiate Venice from Cyprus and that define the particular character of each location as it pertains to the plot of the play.*

2. *Discuss the role of Emilia. How does her character change during the course of the play? Pay particular attention to moments when Emilia decides to be silent and when she decides to speak. What is the effect of her silence about the handkerchief? Do we forgive this silence when she insists on speaking in spite of Iago's threats in the final scene?*

3. *Do a close reading of one of Iago's soliloquies. Point to moments in the language where Iago most gains an audience's sympathy and moments where he most repels it. Pay close attention to the way in which Iago develops arguments about what he must and/or will do. To what extent are these arguments convincing? If they are convincing and an audience's perception of Iago is sympathetic, what happens to its perception of Othello?*

4. *Analyze one or more of the play's bizarre comic scenes: the banter between Iago and Desdemona in Act II, scene i; the drinking song in Act II, scene iii; the clown scenes (Act III, scenes i and iv). How do these scenes echo, reflect, distort, or comment on the more serious matter of the play?*

A+ Student Essay

> Discuss the role that race plays in Shakespeare's portrayal
> of Othello. How do the other characters react to Othello's
> skin color or to the fact that he is a Moor? How does
> Othello see himself?

Othello incurs resentment for many reasons. He is from a land that
Venetians consider exotic and mysterious, he has had unique adventures, and his military accomplishments far exceed those of the men
around him. The most visible indicator of his outsider status is also
the one that provokes the most poisonous responses: Othello is a
black man in white Venice. Whenever characters such as Iago feel
jealousy, fear, or simple hatred toward Othello, they give vent to
their feelings by using racist slurs. For much of the play, Othello
resists, ignores, or seems indifferent to the racism that dogs him.
But eventually he internalizes Iago's and others' idea that his blackness makes him barbarous. This belief, as much as his conviction
of Desdemona's guilt, allows Othello to kill his wife. When he
turns the race weapon against himself, he dooms both himself and
Desdemona.

Among Iago's many repulsive qualities, his eagerness to hurl
racial epithets is perhaps the most shocking. In an attempt to enlist
Brabanzio in his anti-Othello cause, Iago refers to the general as
"the Moor," "the devil," and "a Barbary horse." These terms reduce
Othello to a crude stereotype, turning him into a villain and an animal. When Iago tells Brabanzio that "an old black ram / Is tupping
your white ewe," he demeans a passionate and loving relationship
between two intelligent adults by characterizing Othello as a mind-
less rutting animal who has soiled the pure Desdemona with his
lust. Iago hopes to disgust Brabanzio with this animal imagery and
with the contrast between Othello's blackness and Desdemona's
whiteness.

Like Iago, other Venetians resort to racial slurs to deal with
their own feelings of inferiority or powerlessness. Roderigo, on the
defensive and trying to present himself and Iago as a unified front,
casually refers to Othello as "the thick-lips." This epithet is both
an attempt to undermine Othello's military achievements with a
cheap stereotype as well as a way to pit Roderigo and Iago's physical similarity against Othello's unfamiliar appearance. Brabanzio,

outraged at his daughter's elopement, expresses disbelief that Desdemona could shun the curly-haired young men of Venice in favor of Othello's "sooty bosom." Brabanzio channels his own insecurity about his daughter's loyalty to him by expressing sneering disgust about Othello's race, implying that Othello's blackness is a dirty coating that threatens to soil Desdemona's purity.

While Othello is barraged by racism, he manages to resist its pull for some time. But in Act IV, he crumbles. Othello discusses his race throughout the play—usually in response to something a white Venetian says—but here he makes his first negative reference to it, suggesting that perhaps his blackness is to blame for his lack of conversational ability. It is a quiet moment, but a hugely significant one. It marks a turning point: Othello has fallen victim to the same racist logic (or illogic) that rules the thinking of people such as Iago and Roderigo. Like those men, Othello wants to place the blame for his feelings of inferiority somewhere and winds up laying that blame not where it belongs (in this case, at Iago's feet), but on his own skin. The floodgates have opened, and now Othello is in danger of believing all of Iago's racist nonsense. In the next lines, Othello compares himself to a toad living in a dungeon, as if he has begun to suspect that his blackness makes him a loathsome animal, somehow less than human.

Only when Othello buys into the absurd idea that his race inherently makes him dangerous does he begin to creep toward the possibility of doing violence to his wife. When he sees himself through society's eyes, as a barbaric interloper, Othello begins to despise himself, and it is that self-hatred that allows him to kill what he loves most.

GLOSSARY OF LITERARY TERMS

ANTAGONIST

The entity that acts to frustrate the goals of the *protagonist*. The antagonist is usually another *character* but may also be a non-human force.

ANTIHERO / ANTIHEROINE

A *protagonist* who is not admirable or who challenges notions of what should be considered admirable.

CHARACTER

A person, animal, or any other thing with a personality that appears in a *narrative*.

CLIMAX

The moment of greatest intensity in a text or the major turning point in the *plot*.

CONFLICT

The central struggle that moves the *plot* forward. The conflict can be the *protagonist*'s struggle against fate, nature, society, or another person.

FIRST-PERSON POINT OF VIEW

A literary style in which the *narrator* tells the story from his or her own *point of view* and refers to himself or herself as "I." The narrator may be an active participant in the story or just an observer.

HERO / HEROINE

The principal *character* in a literary work or *narrative*.

IMAGERY

Language that brings to mind sense-impressions, representing things that can be seen, smelled, heard, tasted, or touched.

MOTIF

A recurring idea, structure, contrast, or device that develops or informs the major *themes* of a work of literature.

NARRATIVE

A story.

NARRATOR

The person (sometimes a *character*) who tells a story; the *voice* assumed by the writer. The narrator and the author of the work of literature are not the same person.

PLOT

The arrangement of the events in a story, including the sequence in which they are told, the relative emphasis they are given, and the causal connections between events.

POINT OF VIEW

The *perspective* that a *narrative* takes toward the events it describes.

PROTAGONIST

The main *character* around whom the story revolves.

SETTING

The location of a *narrative* in time and space. Setting creates mood or atmosphere.

SUBPLOT

A secondary *plot* that is of less importance to the overall story but may serve as a point of contrast or comparison to the main plot.

SYMBOL

An object, *character,* figure, or color that is used to represent an abstract idea or concept. Unlike an *emblem,* a symbol may have different meanings in different contexts.

SYNTAX

The way the words in a piece of writing are put together to form lines, phrases, or clauses; the basic structure of a piece of writing.

THEME

A fundamental and universal idea explored in a literary work.

TONE

The author's attitude toward the subject or *characters* of a story or poem or toward the reader.

VOICE

An author's individual way of using language to reflect his or her own personality and attitudes. An author communicates voice through *tone, diction,* and *syntax.*

A NOTE ON PLAGIARISM

Plagiarism—presenting someone else's work as your own—rears its ugly head in many forms. Many students know that copying text without citing it is unacceptable. But some don't realize that even if you're not quoting directly, but instead are paraphrasing or summarizing, *it is plagiarism* unless you cite the source.

Here are the most common forms of plagiarism:

- Using an author's phrases, sentences, or paragraphs without citing the source
- Paraphrasing an author's ideas without citing the source
- Passing off another student's work as your own

How do you steer clear of plagiarism? You should *always* acknowledge all words and ideas that aren't your own by using quotation marks around verbatim text or citations like footnotes and endnotes to note another writer's ideas. For more information on how to give credit when credit is due, ask your teacher for guidance or visit www.sparknotes.com.

Review & Resources

Quiz

1. What pattern is embroidered on the handkerchief?

   A. Strawberries
   B. Dots
   C. Leaves
   D. Daggers

2. How is the Turkish fleet thwarted?

   A. In battle with Othello's fleet
   B. By a storm
   C. Mutiny
   D. In battle with ships from Rhodes

3. What rank does Cassio hold before Othello strips it from him?

   A. Corporal
   B. Private
   C. Lieutenant
   D. Colonel

4. Which of the following animal epithets is not applied to Othello during the play?

   A. Ram
   B. Horse
   C. Serpent
   D. Ass

5. How old is Iago?

   A. Thirty-five
   B. Nineteen
   C. Twenty-eight
   D. Fifty

6. What is "the beast with two backs"?

    A. A mutant horse
    B. Othello
    C. Two people having sex
    D. Conjoined twins

7. What is Brabanzio's position in Venice?

    A. Senator
    B. Duke
    C. Constable
    D. Stable-hand

8. Where does Iago tell Roderigo that Othello and Desdemona are sailing to from Cyprus?

    A. Morocco
    B. America
    C. Crete
    D. Mauritania

9. Who made the handkerchief that Othello inherited from his mother?

    A. Barbary
    B. Othello's mother
    C. Othello's former lover
    D. A sibyl, or female prophet

10. What first attracted Desdemona to Othello?

    A. His strong hands
    B. His beautifully crafted armor
    C. His handkerchief
    D. The stories he told about his past

11. What rank does Iago begrudgingly hold?

    A. Colonel
    B. Sergeant
    C. Ensign
    D. Captain

REVIEW & RESOURCES

12. From whom did Desdemona first hear the "song of 'Willow'"?

    A. Othello
    B. Her mother's maid, Barbary
    C. The clown
    D. Emilia

13. Which of the following epithets is most commonly applied to Iago throughout the play?

    A. "Honest"
    B. "Fat"
    C. "Stubborn"
    D. "Ugly"

14. Whose death does Graziano report in the final scene?

    A. The duke's
    B. Lodovico's
    C. Bianca's
    D. Brabanzio's

15. Which of Cassio's weaknesses does Iago exploit?

    A. His inability to ride a horse
    B. A low tolerance for alcohol
    C. A bad knee
    D. A short attention span

16. Whom does Iago refer to as the true general?

    A. The duke
    B. Brabanzio
    C. Desdemona
    D. Lodovico

17. How does Othello kill Desdemona?

    A. He stabs her.
    B. He smothers her.
    C. He strangles her.
    D. He beats her to death.

18. What, according to Iago, is the "green-eyed monster"?

    A. Envy
    B. Greed
    C. Sexual desire
    D. Jealousy

19. Whom does Cassio wound in the drunken brawl of Act II, scene iii?

    A. Roderigo
    B. Iago
    C. Montano
    D. Graziano

20. With whom does Cassio dine the night he is stabbed?

    A. Othello
    B. Lodovico
    C. Desdemona
    D. Bianca

21. What is Othello holding as he stands over the sleeping Desdemona?

    A. A light
    B. A sword
    C. A flower
    D. A pillow

22. Who is the first character to refer to Othello by name?

    A. The duke
    B. Iago
    C. Brabanzio
    D. Desdemona

23. According to Lodovico's letter, who is to replace Othello as governor of Cyprus?

    A. Montano
    B. Cassio
    C. Iago
    D. Lodovico

24. On the night of her death, what does Desdemona ask Emilia to do?

    A. Put ribbons in Desdemona's hair
    B. Sing Desdemona to sleep
    C. Put Desdemona's wedding sheets on the bed
    D. Embroider Desdemona a new handkerchief

25. What does Iago counsel Roderigo to do?

    A. "Put seeds in thy garden"
    B. "Put money in thy purse"
    C. "Put woman out of thy mind"
    D. "Put thy head upon my shoulder"

SUGGESTIONS FOR FURTHER READING

BRADBROOK, MURIEL C. *Themes and Conventions in Elizabethan Drama*. Cambridge: Cambridge University Press, 2nd edition 2002.

BRADLEY, A. C. *Shakespearean Tragedy: Lectures on* HAMLET, OTHELLO, KING LEAR, & MACBETH. New York: Palgrave Macmillan, 2007.

CAVELL, STANLEY. *Disowning Knowledge in Six Plays of Shakespeare*. Cambridge: Cambridge University Press, 1987.

GURR, ANDREW. *The Shakespearean Stage, 1574–1642*. Cambridge: Cambridge University Press, 1992.

HEILMAN, ROBERT. *Magic in the Web: Action and Language in* OTHELLO. Lexington: University of Kentucky Press, 1956.

KOLIN, PHILIP, ed. OTHELLO: *New Critical Essays*. New York: Routledge, 2001.

ROSENBERG, MARVIN. *The Masks of Othello*. Newark, DE: University of Delaware Press, new edition 1992.

SHAUGHNESSY, ROBERT, ed. *Shakespeare in Performance*. New York: St. Martin's Press, 2000.

SNYDER, SUSAN. OTHELLO: *Critical Essays*. New York: Garland, 1988.

VAUGHAN, VIRGINIA MASON. OTHELLO: *A Contextual History*. New York: Cambridge University Press, 1997.

SparkNotes Literature Guides

1984
The Adventures of
  Huckleberry Finn
The Adventures of
  Tom Sawyer
The Aeneid
All Quiet on the
  Western Front
And Then There Were
  None
Angela's Ashes
Animal Farm
Anna Karenina
Anne of Green Gables
Anthem
As I Lay Dying
The Awakening
The Bean Trees
Beloved
Beowulf
Billy Budd
Black Boy
Bless Me, Ultima
The Bluest Eye
Brave New World
The Brothers
  Karamazov
The Call of the Wild
Candide
The Canterbury Tales
Catch-22
The Catcher in the Rye
The Chocolate War
The Chosen
Cold Sassy Tree
The Color Purple
The Count of Monte
  Cristo
Crime and Punishment
The Crucible
Cry, the Beloved
  Country
Cyrano de Bergerac
David Copperfield
Death of a Salesman
Death of Socrates
Diary of a Young Girl

A Doll's House
Don Quixote
Dr. Faustus
Dr. Jekyll and Mr. Hyde
Dracula
Edith Hamilton's
  Mythology
Emma
Ethan Frome
Fahrenheit 451
A Farewell to Arms
The Fellowship of the
  Rings
Flowers for Algernon
For Whom the Bell
  Tolls
The Fountainhead
Frankenstein
The Giver
The Glass Menagerie
The Good Earth
The Grapes of Wrath
Great Expectations
The Great Gatsby
Grendel
Gulliver's Travels
Hamlet
The Handmaid's Tale
Hard Times
Heart of Darkness
Henry IV, Part I
Henry V
Hiroshima
The Hobbit
The House on Mango
  Street
I Know Why the Caged
  Bird Sings
The Iliad
The Importance of
  Being Earnest
Inferno
Invisible Man
Jane Eyre
Johnny Tremain
The Joy Luck Club
Julius Caesar

The Jungle
The Killer Angels
King Lear
The Last of the
  Mohicans
Les Misérables
A Lesson Before Dying
Little Women
Lord of the Flies
Macbeth
Madame Bovary
The Merchant of
  Venice
A Midsummer Night's
  Dream
Moby-Dick
Much Ado About
  Nothing
My Ántonia
Narrative of the Life of
  Frederick Douglass
Native Son
The New Testament
Night
The Odyssey
Oedipus Plays
Of Mice and Men
The Old Man and
  the Sea
The Old Testament
Oliver Twist
The Once and Future
  King
One Flew Over the
  Cuckoo's Nest
One Hundred Years of
  Solitude
Othello
Our Town
The Outsiders
Paradise Lost
The Pearl
The Picture of Dorian
  Gray
Poe's Short Stories
A Portrait of the Artist
  as a Young Man

Pride and Prejudice
The Prince
A Raisin in the Sun
The Red Badge of
  Courage
The Republic
The Return of the King
Richard III
Robinson Crusoe
Romeo and Juliet
Scarlet Letter
A Separate Peace
Silas Marner
Sir Gawain and the
  Green Knight
Slaughterhouse-Five
Song of Solomon
The Sound and the
  Fury
The Stranger
A Streetcar Named
  Desire
The Sun Also Rises
A Tale of Two Cities
The Taming of the
  Shrew
The Tempest
Tess of the
  d'Urbervilles
The Things They
  Carried
The Two Towers
Their Eyes Were
  Watching God
Things Fall Apart
To Kill a Mockingbird
Treasure Island
Twelfth Night
Ulysses
Uncle Tom's Cabin
Walden
War and Peace
Wuthering Heights
A Yellow Raft in Blue
  Water

Visit sparknotes.com for many more!